FLORATOPIA

———

FLORATOPIA

110 Flower Garden Ideas for Your Yard, Patio, or Balcony

JAN JOHNSEN

The Countryman Press

A Division of W. W. Norton & Company

Independent Publishers Since 1923

Copyright © 2021 by Jan Johnsen

For information about permission to reproduce selections from this book, write to
Permissions, The Countryman Press, 500 Fifth Avenue, New York, NY 10110

For information about special discounts for bulk purchases, please contact
W. W. Norton Special Sales at specialsales@wwnorton.com or 800-233-4830

Manufacturing by ToppanLeefung
Book design by Allison Chi
Production manager: Devon Zahn

Library of Congress Cataloging-in-Publication Data

Names: Johnsen, Jan, author.
Title: Floratopia : 110 flower garden ideas for your yard, patio,
or balcony / Jan Johnsen.
Description: New York, NY : The Countryman Press, [2021] | Includes index.
Identifiers: LCCN 2020039272 | ISBN 9781682685983 (hardcover) | ISBN
9781682685990 (epub)
Subjects: LCSH: Flower gardening.
Classification: LCC SB405 .J57 2021 | DDC 635.9—dc23
LC record available at https://lccn.loc.gov/2020039272

The Countryman Press
www.countrymanpress.com

A division of W. W. Norton & Company, Inc.
500 Fifth Avenue, New York, NY 10110
www.wwnorton.com

978-1-68268-598-3

10 9 8 7 6 5 4 3 2 1

For flower lovers everywhere, who revel in Nature's gorgeous gifts.

May you plant flowers wherever you are and whenever you want.

Contents

Introduction

———

"People from a planet without flowers would think we must
be mad with joy the whole time to have such things about us."
—IRIS MURDOCH

Flowers are, unquestionably, the jewels of the green world. Their sole task is to become pollinated and produce fruit and seeds, but it is the colorful and fragrant way they go about this task that captivates us. We cannot help but look in wonder at the perfection of a daisy, an iris, or a poppy. As the British novelist Iris Murdoch noted, we should be mad with joy to have flowers about us. Of course, many flowers are short-lived and seasonal, which makes them even more beguiling. A spring morning is exalted by the all-too-brief display of tulips and daffodils. A summer evening is enhanced by the subtle fragrance of nicotiana and twining honeysuckle. And who cannot be gladdened by a slightly wilted posy of wildflowers gripped by the fingers of a smiling child?

The siren call of flowers is indeed hard to resist. And they are such an important part of our living world—offering food and habitat to our threatened pollinators such as bees, birds, butterflies, and more. That is why I chose to write about flowers and flower garden design. I have worked with flowers as a landscape designer and horticulturist all my adult life, and I know how wonderful it is to open the door to the sight of colorful blooms in the garden. More important, I believe we need flower gardens—our pollinator havens—more than ever. The more flowers we plant, the happier our endangered pollinators will be.

Flowers should play a bigger part in the modern world we live in because they brighten everyone's mood. I wrote *Floratopia* to help in that effort. In the following pages, I profile flowers that anyone can grow. I discuss which flowers work well together for the best effect and share a few "secrets" for helping them thrive. And I spotlight some of my favorite flowers. I hope these tips inspire you to try your hand at growing flowers in a pot or in a plant bed. Or, if you do that already, to plant a flower or two that is new to you. This book is a paean to flower gardening, in all its guises.

Flowers have always been valued for their beautiful colors, fragrance, and form; but now, thanks to the influence of plantsman Piet Oudolf and other current landscape designers, we are learning to appreciate flowers' seed heads and winter interest as well. In *Floratopia*, I note the trend to "intermingle" plants that flower and mature at different times. The seed heads of one flower sit side by side with another type that is just beginning to blossom. This expanded appreciation takes us beyond bright colors of spring and summer and into the earthy browns of late fall. It highlights flowers' inherent beauty in all seasons.

Floratopia also stresses the vital role that flowers play in sustainable and eco-friendly gardens. The dance between flowers and their pollinators such as bees, moths, hummingbirds, butterflies, and birds is a crucial biological function. Flower gardens are really all about the pollinators. By planting a flower garden, not only do we enjoy its beauty, but we also create a habitat that can

Above: Pink coneflowers (*Echinacea*) and 'Summer Nights' oxeye sunflower (*Heliopsis helianthoides* 'Summer Nights') form an exuberant summer-blooming perennial duo. The coneflowers begin to bloom in early summer while the oxeye sunflowers start flowering in mid-summer. Both are native plants and will continue blooming into autumn, especially if deadheaded. 'Summer Nights' has goldeny-yellow, daisy-like blooms with mahogany centers. Hardy to zones 3–9. This is at the outstanding public garden, Chanticleer, in Wayne, Pennsylvania.

Left: *Papaver orientale*, the oriental poppy, is native to Turkey and the Caucasus Mountains. The dark color at the heart of some oriental poppies mimics the presence of a female beetle, which is meant to attract pollinating male beetles in their native regions. A dwarf variety, 'Allegro' Oriental poppy (*Papaver orientale* 'Allegro') has scarlet-orange blooms with a dark center. It grows 18 to 24 inches tall and blooms in late spring-early summer; zones 3–8.

offer areas for egg laying and overwintering, for hosting butterfly larvae, and of course, for feeding. To paraphrase a well-known saying, "If you plant it, they will come."

And lastly, *Floratopia* shares design ideas and growing techniques to help you create the flower garden of your dreams. I had the good fortune to learn these skills from a master French gardener, Alain Grumberg, years ago. He had trained in the world-famous gardens of Versailles before coming to the United States to become the head of grounds at Mohonk Mountain House, the historic resort hotel in New Paltz, New York. I worked in the display gardens there and, under Alain's direction, we grew thousands of annual flowering plants from seed and planted them out in prepared flower beds in late May. We used European organic gardening methods—no pesticides or chemical fertilizers.

In the ensuing years, I have designed and supervised the planting of many flower gardens for clients around the country. I also plant flowers in containers and raised beds. One thing I have learned is that you do not need to have a grand garden—a simple planter full of flowers or a small flower bed is enough to feel the contentment that British writer A. A. Milne described so eloquently: "Flowers give a prolonged delight to all, both in the garden and out of it; and though one can buy cut flowers, one cannot buy the happiness which they give us as they grow."

Flowers growing around us supply us with a sublime happiness. That is why *Floratopia* focuses on relatively fast-growing herbaceous flowering plants. The term *herbaceous* means a plant that has soft green stems. I do not cover flowers that grow on woody shrubs or trees like roses, lilacs, and hydrangeas in this book. However, there is so much to discuss when it comes to herbaceous flowers.

ORGANIZATION OF THE BOOK

Floratopia is a book of individual illustrated tips and suggestions meant to stimulate your interest in flower gardening. There are six chapters and a total of 110 numbered tips. I aim to entice you to try some of these plants and ideas in your outdoor space, no matter the size. I answer questions like, "I like purple and silver, so what should I grow?" or "What are some varieties of *Baptisia* to try?" or "Which hardy perennials are deer resistant?" *Floratopia* is not a detailed growing manual, so if you are interested in growing any of the plants profiled here or trying ideas that I suggest, I hope you will research their specific growing requirements further.

The first chapter, Flowers in Pots & Planters, centers on the trend of growing plants in containers. We all love pots overflowing with flowers, and it is easy to begin your foray into gardening with

Here I am at work—don't go on your knees when you plant out flowers. Kneeling compacts the soil and prevents you from moving easily; instead, straddle the bed or stand beside it and bend, if you can.

planters. The popularity of container gardening is due to its ease and versatility—you can place containers anywhere. This section highlights flowers that work well in containers and gives tips on growing them in planters.

The second chapter, Flower Garden Planting Tips, addresses the hands-on aspect of flower gardening. I share pointers for preparing flower beds and growing flowers successfully. I explain USDA Plant Hardiness Zones (pages 76–77), tools to use, and more. These are general techniques that I use when out in the field. The tips can help make gardening tasks more enjoyable.

The third chapter, Flower Garden Design Tips & Green Thoughts, addresses what many gardeners love to discuss—the design and use of flowers in a garden. I refer to color, texture, and height, and suggest flower combinations to try as well. I also share a few of my musings about the benefits of flowers and gardening in our lives. I call those my "green thoughts."

The fourth chapter, Themes for Flower Gardens, is for people who love concept gardens that celebrate a color, an insect, a natural condition, a historic period, and more. Flower gardens let you do that in such a beautiful way. I hope the themes I suggest get your creative juices flowing! I am sure there are many other themes that I have not thought of, so this chapter is just a starting point.

The fifth chapter, A Few Choice Perennial Flowers to Try, spotlights some easy-care perennial plants that I especially like. These popular flowering plants bloom during a certain season, go dormant in winter, and return the following year. Their reliable emergence from the ground every spring makes them the most desirable type of flowers to many gardeners. I feature a few select perennials that I have found to be great performers, attract pollinators, and are easy to grow. I also suggest companion plants.

The sixth and last chapter, A Selection of Favorite Annual Flowers, highlights some great performing annuals. Annuals are flowers that bloom consistently all season but do not come back the next year. I love annual flowers and have planted them in all kinds of landscapes—among perennials, ferns, rocks, and more. In this section, I share just a few special favorites. I discuss new varieties to try and ideas for combining them with other flowers.

This book has been a labor of love for me. Most of the photographs are mine and are of gardens and flowers I have planted through the years while working as a designer/horticulturist. I focus on flowers that grow in cooler areas rather than in southern or subtropical hardiness zones. Many that I discuss are suitable to a wide range of hardiness zones.

I hope that *Floratopia* inspires you to try your hand at growing flowers. I think you will find that they elevate the atmosphere, help our pollinators, and add a bit of joy to your outdoor space, wherever it may be. As botanist Luther Burbank said, "Flowers always make people better, happier, and more helpful; they are sunshine, food, and medicine for the soul."

A cacophony of tulips greets spring in a most colorful way. A client, and dear friend, planted this mass of colorful tulip bulbs in the fall. What a way to start out the gardening year!

"'Just living is not enough,' said the butterfly,
'one must have sunshine, freedom, and a little flower.'"
—HANS CHRISTIAN ANDERSEN

FLOWERS IN POTS & PLANTERS

No matter where you live, you can enjoy flowers planted in containers. Growing flowers in pots, planters, or even old wheelbarrows (!) satisfies that longing we all have for Nature's most colorful and fragrant creations. Hans Christian Andersen was right when he said that we must have a little flower. And you can delight in having flowers in pots even if you have a small balcony or patio.

I know how satisfying it is to grow some greenery in unlikely spaces. When I was a child in Brooklyn, New York, I longed to grow something, and so I grew plants in large tomato sauce cans on our fire escape. We lived on the top floor and I saw it as my little garden in the sky. I punched drainage holes in the bottom of the cans with a screwdriver. I filled them with soil from a neighbor's yard and planted them up. It wasn't the best technique, but it worked. I had my prized marigolds, tomatoes, and coleus sitting outside my window.

Outdoor container gardening makes eminent sense if you are a flower lover. Growing in planters and pots allows you to enjoy flowers and help in the effort to feed our endangered pollinators. All you need is some high-quality potting mix, a suitable container, and a few small plants. With these you can have a colorful display on a terrace, deck, balcony, or outdoors in the garden. You may start with a pot or two of petunias and then add a geranium, and slowly it might become an obsession. Ask any gardener and they will tell you that planters, overflowing with vegetation, are like rabbits—they seem to multiply overnight. Soon, you will have planters on your porch or balcony, alongside the driveway, on your entry steps, and even placed within plant beds.

The art of growing plants in outdoor planters—especially flowers—has come a long way since the late 1960s and the introduction of specialized "soil" mixes formulated for growing plants in containers. Those potting mixes were lightweight, offered good aeration, and were able to hold ample moisture for plant growth. The ability to fill large outdoor pots with a uniform and sterile "soil" mix transformed what was a small gardening practice into what is now a big part of the horticultural industry. Today, there are many potting mixes for growing all kinds of plants. The mixes are reliable and consistent. Some contain slow-release fertilizer and others are organically based with earthworm castings, compost, and much more. These mixes make the task of growing big blooms in a planter easy.

This chapter offers tips and suggestions for creating beautiful planters full of herbaceous (soft-stemmed) flowers—both perennial and annuals. The photos I share are meant to spark ideas for growing your own floral paradise in containers. If a specific plant that I suggest catches your fancy, please look for more information about it in catalogs, magazines, or the Internet. Some of the photos shown here are from gardens I designed for clients, and many planter combinations were created by the exceptional garden center, Michael's Garden Gate Nursery, in Mount Kisco, New York.

Planters full of flowers add a sublime, life-giving energy to any space. They can help our pollinators and give us joy at the same time. In this chapter, I aim to inspire you to try your hand at growing flowers in planters and pots so that you can join in the fun, no matter where you live.

The myriad colors of annual flowers is on display in this planter. The unique bicolor blooms of Supertunia® 'Pretty Much Picasso' is on the right, trailing over the edge. It has a deep violet throat with lighter violet petals edged with a chartreuse border. The star-shaped, light blue flowers in the center are long-blooming blue stars (*Laurentia axillaris*).

Lavender fan flowers (*Scaevola aemula*) overhang the side of a metal urn. This easy-care annual flower in a raised container adds a colorful touch to a landscape of ornamental grasses.

Opposite page: Looking like small orchids, Nemesia, an annual flower, hangs over a pot in spring. With a rainbow of colors available, Nemesia is a great addition to any cool-season container or garden. Heat-tolerant cultivars and beautiful bicolor blooms are available. Plant with pansies, violas, and white alyssum for a wonderful spring planter.

1. THE CLASSIC—GERANIUMS IN POTS

What is the most common flower grown outdoors in pots? Without a doubt, it must be geraniums. These showy flowers have long been gracing our front stoops, window boxes, and gardens. It is easy to see why they are so popular—geraniums can turn a simple planter into a brilliant pop of summer color with their impressive blooms.

The zonal geranium, as it is called, is really a pelargonium. It is *Pelargonium × hortorum* to be exact. The name mix-up goes back to when pelargoniums were introduced to Europe from South Africa in the 1600s. Back then, they were misclassified as a geranium. This was corrected later but the common name stuck, and we continue to call it a geranium. It is called zonal due to the markings or zones that may be found on its round leaves.

Zonal geraniums are tropical perennials, hardy in USDA hardiness zones 10–12, that are grown as annual flowers in cooler regions. They are a very easy flower to grow. Geraniums bloom best in sun (they may require some shade in hot areas) and benefit from a diluted liquid bloom booster fertilizer every few weeks. They do not require a lot of water, and care should be taken not to overwater them (important tip). Deadhead the flower stalks for continued blooms all summer into fall.

Intense red is the classic geranium color, but modern hybrid blooms come in shades of pink, salmon, lavender, yellow, orange, white, and rose. Interestingly, geraniums can be trained to grow as standards. Standards are small tree forms with a straight woody stem and a round top full of foliage and flowers. These small "lollipop" geranium trees are outstanding in a classic planter, especially when surrounded by lower growing plants such as creeping Jenny (*Lysimachia nummularia*) and creeping blue sedum (*Sedum sieboldii*). For instant elegance, plant a geranium tree in a pot and place on either side of a sunny front door.

Left: Red and pink zonal geraniums, along with silvery dusty miller and white African cape daisy (*Osteospermum ecklonis*), kick off early summer in a container with style. Add some Techno Blue lobelia or blue petunias and you have a planter that will be patriotic all summer.

Opposite page: The red geranium (*Pelargonium × hortorum*) is so prevalent in some European countries that it could be considered their signature flower. Here, they are at the US home of a Swiss friend of mine, Maya Manley. She never fails to plant red geraniums (always red) in terracotta pots along the length of her raised terrace.

2. THE REMARKABLE CALIBRACHOA— A CONTAINER STAR

Calibrachoa (ca-libra-KO-a) is not a name that rolls off the tongue. So, many people refer to this popular tender perennial as Million Bells® or Superbells® due to the many miniature petunia-like blooms that line its trailing stems. This profuse bloomer sports small jewel-like flowers in a rainbow variety of colors, and you have probably seen it in containers and hanging baskets. Calibrachoa flowers appear in every tone of color, and you can find cultivars with striped and star patterns, dark eyes, or single or double blooms. Their intricate color combinations are truly remarkable. This outstanding flowering plant is grown as an annual in areas colder than USDA hardiness zones 9–11.

Few types of plants have experienced the kind of "overnight success" that calibrachoa has. It first came on the market in the early 1990s as Million Bells®, growing beautifully in hanging baskets and pots. It is now one of the most popular annual flowers sold each year. The reasons for its phenomenal success as a container plant is its range of color combinations, easy-care status (no deadheading!), and heat tolerance and durability. In fact, the National Garden Bureau proclaimed 2018 as the Year of the Calibrachoa.

This sun-loving trailer is a great choice for sunny pots and window boxes. Its fleshy stems, which grow 6 to 15 inches long, are covered with a multitude of flowers that spill loosely over the edge. Calibrachoa plants will grow in five hours of sun and more. Fertilizing ensures more flowers. Mix in a slow-release fertilizer at planting and, later on, apply a diluted solution of liquid fertilizer every few weeks. If the plants start to get leggy, meaning that it starts to grow long stems, do not be afraid to clip them back hard to encourage new growth.

Top, left: Calibrachoa Superbells® 'Hollywood Star' trails over a pot in rose-pink splendor, its bright yellow throat outlined as a special effect. This flower does not fade even in the heat of summer.

Top, right: The bicolor calibrachoa Superbells® 'Lemon Slice' spills over the edge of a red-brown pot, growing along with white mini-impatiens and the deep burgundy coleus ColorBlaze® 'Marooned' (*Plectranthus scutellarioides* ColorBlaze® 'Marooned'). The pinwheel pattern of slices of yellow and white on the petals makes this cultivar of calibrachoa a real standout!

Bottom, left: Close up of calibrachoa Superbells® 'Lemon Slice.' Although calibrachoa is a sun lover, it will grow almost as well in partial shade.

Bottom, right: Fun fact—Calibrachoa is native to Chile, Peru, and southern Brazil. It is named for Antonio de la Cal y Bracho (1766–1833), a Spanish-born Mexican pharmacist and botanist. The calibrachoas shown here can use a little trim to increase branching and create a fuller look. Use a sharp pair of scissors or pruning shears, and feel free to clip away often.

3. SO MANY PLANTERS TO CHOOSE FROM!

The rise in popularity of planters and planter gardening reflects how our lifestyles have changed. Downsizing to a smaller home or enjoying an urban lifestyle means living in more compact spaces. Planters are the answer for many small space dwellers. Instead of in-the-ground gardens, we choose to be surrounded with planters of all sizes on small patios, decks, and porches. We can change out the seasonal display easily and move plants around, and we can remain standing (or sitting) while tending to our flowers. Planter gardening is also a great introduction

Neutral colors, a rounded shape, and a lightweight, resin-based material makes this planter a popular item! Its muted, natural appearance works well with any style. Best of all, it can remain outside all winter. Use a 14-inch diameter, or larger, for the best displays. Large containers also require less frequent watering.

to growing all kinds of plants. People who don't think of themselves as gardeners often change their mind as they become enamored with the planting combinations they create in a simple planter or container.

Years back, the available planter styles were limited. Today, the variety of plant containers is tremendous, thanks to global trade and advances in manufacturing. Of course, too much choice makes it hard to pick out just one planter. Your preferences for style, cost, weight, and maintenance should be your ultimate guide. You can choose stylish, modern pots featuring geometric shapes; classic urns; casual cottage-style planters; and many others. If you want your house and landscape to have a cohesive look, choose a style that matches your decor. Or you can add several modern planters to update your surroundings and give it a trendy feel. Mix and match is totally allowed, which is another reason why gardening in planters is so fun.

My suggestion is to consider weight and winter durability, first. Planters, especially those on the larger size, can become quite heavy once filled with soil and plants. If your planter is destined for a 10th-floor balcony, or if you have to lug the planter up some steps, heavy pots will present you with a challenge. Likewise, if your pots cannot withstand subfreezing temperatures, then you will have to empty them out and store them somewhere. If that is your situation, I suggest you consider using durable lightweight planters made from a resin-based material that can stay in place outside through the winter. They come in all sizes and styles. They may be more costly, but the convenience is worth it in the long run.

A friend and client of mine, Danielle, loves to grow flowers in pots. She mixes colors and textures beautifully. Her display of planters adds height and interest and extends her lovely garden onto her terrace. An avid container gardener changes the flower display every season.

A classic cast-stone urn such as this one is beautiful even if it is empty! Here it is placed in a garden bed surrounded by white sweet alyssum. Make certain the planter has a drainage hole to let rainwater out.

Want to jazz up your patio? These ceramic planters have an artful, abstract-glazed finish and are constructed from weather-resistant material. They tolerate bright UV sun rays well.

Terracotta planters are made from terracotta clay that's been fired at a high temperature. In fact, the word *terracotta* comes from the Italian words for "baked earth." Some top-quality terracotta planters are frost proof but don't assume that—ask the vendor to be sure.

Vintage pots in popular earthy textures and tones make quite a statement in the landscape. These are at Inner Gardens in Los Angeles. It is well worth a visit for any planter lover.

4. TROPICAL PLANTERS—WHY NOT?

You want to go away to a tropical island without leaving home? Why not plant up several tropical-themed outdoor pots and enjoy a staycation? Add some tiki torches and string some twinkly lights and voila! You have a tropical backyard paradise. And it all starts with the planters.

Tropical-themed planters have a central plant that is suited to hot and humid climates. These are normally large-leaved plants that seem to outgrow the pot, which is what can happen. If you want to go with a tropical theme, always choose a large heavy pot that will support a tall plant and its extensive roots. Place a large stone or two in the bottom for added weight. This will prevent the container from tipping over in a wind gust.

One plant that fits the tropical theme well is the colorful and flamboyant canna lily (*Canna × generalis*). Its bold, banana-leaved foliage makes a strong impact and its flowers come in an array of vibrant colors. Canna lilies are subtropical and tropical plants (USDA hardiness zones 8–11) that require full sun and rich, moist soil. You can buy young canna plants and pot them in a large container. Or you can buy canna rhizomes (these are similar to bulbs) and plant directly in a planter. Bury the rhizome, horizontally, 2 inches deep in the soil, with the eye facing up. Space the rhizomes 12 to 18 inches apart. Water thoroughly and often. Cannas love water. They are also heavy feeders and will bloom more profusely with applications of fertilizer in early spring and midsummer. Make sure the planter is large to accommodate the roots.

Another choice for a sculptural tropical plant in a large pot is the dramatic elephant ears (*Colocasia*) with its giant heart-shaped leaves. There are many cultivars to choose from—some with purplish-black leaves or purple and green foliage. In full sun the plant may be more compact, and in lower light the leaf stems will grow longer, making the plant look more airy.

Top, left: The striped foliage of large-leaved canna lilies set the tropical tone for a pool area. Canna lilies are known for their striking foliage; they come in a wide range of colors and patterns. The dark pink petunias, an annual, are a nice contrast to the cannas, and light green sweet potato vine (*Ipomoea batatas*) spills over exuberantly.

Top, right: Large canna leaves in the middle of a planter can act as an umbrella and prevent light rain from reaching the soil below. The water lands on the large leaves and sheds right off. When you are watering, make sure you apply water beneath the leaves. Also, wait to see water seeping out from the drainage holes in the bottom of the pot to be sure you applied enough. Here, the luxuriant and resilient blooms of the annual flower 'Homestead Purple' Verbena (*Verbena canadensis* 'Homestead Purple') fall over the sides of the planter. 'Homestead Purple' Verbena is a vigorous, low-growing plant that spreads out easily in a single growing season.

Bottom, left: The extra-large, beautiful leaves of the bird of paradise plant (*Strelitzia reginae*) are unmistakable. Its orange and blue blooms (not shown) look like the head of an exotic crested bird, thus its common name. It lends a tropical feeling to any setting. If the pot is big enough, bird of paradise can grow to 5 feet tall. It grows in bright sunlight. In shade, the foliage is healthy but blooming decreases. Zones 9–11. Here, the red pendant flowers of begonia 'Bonfire' (*Begonia boliviensis* 'Bonfire') dangle delicately over the edge of the planter.

Bottom, right: Tropical hibiscus flowers (*Hibiscus rosa-sinensis*) make great summer accents in pots. They need full sun to thrive. The bold, plate-shaped flowers come in shades of red, pink, yellow, orange, purple, and white. Tropical hibiscus are summer-blooming plants that grow well in containers. Beautiful for patios, decks, and balconies. Go with dwarf hibiscus for planters, which grow 2–4 feet tall. Standard varieties typically grow up to 5 feet tall.

5. DRAINAGE IN POTS—NEW RECOMMENDATIONS

Filling planters and pots with bagged potting mix is not difficult. The tricky part is to ensure proper drainage at the bottom of the container. The standard practice has always been to fill the base of pots with a layer of gravel or stones for drainage. It was time-consuming but we were told it was important. Recently, the recommendations have changed! Life is now simpler for the container gardener.

Scientists have found that water moving down through a pot will not easily go from potting mix into a coarser material like gravel. The water remains in the mix portion and does not seep down. Why? Because water does not pass quickly from one material into another material that has a different pore (opening) size. In other words, gravel and stones actually hinder the movement of water down through the pot. The water tends to stay in the potting mix layer.

The suggestion now is simply to fill the pot with potting mix. For optimal drainage in your planters, make sure there are drainage holes in the base (important!). You may choose to cover the holes with mesh to prevent soil from washing out. You can make your own mesh by using a netted bag that holds fruit. Simply cut a small piece of the plastic mesh and place it at the bottom of the pot before filling with mix.

If you have a large planter, in the bottom-third of the pot place one or two lightweight bulky items that don't rot, such as clean, empty plastic milk jugs or soda bottles. This saves on potting mix and makes the pot less heavy. If you have a large container in which you intend to plant annual flowers, the bottom of the pot can be filled with chunky bark mulch. This last tip works with annual flowers because they have shorter root systems than perennials or tropical plants.

Once the pot is filled, compact the mix around the inside of the rim. Just use your hand pointing downward. This is the area where the most compaction is needed. Never compact the potting mix too much in the center, because then the water cannot pass through.

Bagged potting soil, begonias, and coleus are all you need for a great-looking planter in the shade. Fill the planter completely with the potting soil—no drainage materials needed at the base! Note that the planter is "footed," which means it is raised off the ground. This helps with drainage.

6. POTTING MIX AND FEEDING—SO IMPORTANT

Plant your flowers in planters filled with quality potting mix. The right potting mix ensures your success! I know bagged mixes may be costly, but they offer a consistent balance of water retention, drainage, and aeration. Never use the soil from your garden in your containers. It is too heavy for a contained space. The roots of herbaceous flowers need a light and fluffy potting mix.

Quality potting soil does not normally contain actual soil, which is why we refer to it as a potting mix. Many potting mixes are made up of peat moss, pine bark, and perlite or vermiculite. More and more potting mixes are compost-based, designed specifically for growing in planters. If you want a potting mix formulated from natural ingredients, there are quite a few to choose from. They can include substances such as earthworm castings, mycorrhizae, bat guano, and fish and crab meal.

Healthy, disease-resistant container plants appreciate occasional applications of plant food. Some potting mixes contain slow-release fertilizers that feed the flowers over a long period. You can add starter mix fertilizer (organic starter fertilizer is now available) to the potting mix when you first plant up the pot. You can also feed your plants with diluted solutions of liquid plant food. This fertilizer can be chemical based or organic based, depending on your preference. I am a proponent of fish emulsion, compost tea, and seaweed-based soil additives.

I usually feed plants in containers with a liquid fertilizer or compost tea a few weeks after planting. A lot of plants in a contained space need more nutrition than if they were in the ground. Be sure to follow the manufacturer's directions for using liquid fertilizer. If there is a lot of rain, fertilizers will wash away in the water, meaning you may need to apply more often.

Slow-release fertilizers are helpful fertilizers and can be applied every six to eight weeks. This is a timesaver and reduces the runoff of excess fertilizer into the soil. Slow-release fertilizer can be added to the soil at the time of planting and during the season. It is wrapped in a hard shell so it lasts and lasts.

A word of warning—do not overfeed your flowering plants! Moderation is the key. Too much fertilizer can "burn" your plants, which means plants cannot take up water. Overfed plants are also more susceptible to insects and disease. Plants are like us: we perform better when we are not too full or too hungry. Less is better than too much when it comes to feeding your plants.

"The Amen of nature is
always a flower."
—OLIVER WENDELL
HOLMES SR.

7. BEGGING FOR BEGONIAS

Begonias were once thought to be an old-fashioned flower, but no more. The small, dainty wax begonia has been replaced in the hearts of planter lovers by bolder hybrids such as Dragon Wing begonias. This remarkable hybrid is a cross between angel wing begonias and wax begonias. It features 5-inch-long, deep, glossy-green, wing-shaped leaves, hanging stems, and large drooping clusters of flowers. The flowers come in shades of red, pink, and white and keep blooming from spring to frost. These vigorous plants do best with morning sun and light afternoon shade. The large plants grow 18 inches across and are well suited for planters or hanging baskets.

Additionally, you can try the BIG series of hybrid begonia, which is part angel wing, part fibrous begonia. They are bushy and have a more upright habit, growing 20 inches tall and wide. It is heavy blooming and holds 2- to 3-inch blooms above green, glossy leaves. This popular begonia blooms from early summer to late summer and withstands summer heat. The BIG begonia series has combinations of red flower with green leaf, red with bronze leaf, and rose with bronze leaf. BIG begonias put on a show in large containers in part sun to part shade.

A unique cultivar is the 'Canary Wings' begonia. It produces dark red blossoms but with wing-shaped, chartreuse leaves! The glowing foliage brightens up shady corners and is ideal for hanging baskets and containers. 'Canary Wings' was named one of the Best New Annuals of 2018 by *Garden Gate* magazine.

In the summer months, hybrid begonias are attention-grabbing in any kind of container. They bloom under a variety of light conditions, but they do best in light shade. They need well-drained soil, at least 50-percent humidity, and warm temperatures to be at their best. They may be grown as a perennial in humid USDA hardiness zones 10–11.

Top: Red Dragon Wing begonias flourish in this low rectangular container. I plant them here every year—in a partly shady spot—for a constant and striking bloom next to the front door. In deeper shade, they have a looser habit and bloom less generously.

Bottom: The BIG Red hybrid begonia, shown here with trailing variegated ivy, is an early bloomer with red flowers held above large, glossy green foliage. It blooms all summer in sun or shade. Perfect for containers, the BIG series of begonias are self-cleaning—no deadheading required. Here, the dark red-brown planters set off the green-and-white ivy foliage effectively.

8. YELLOW PETUNIAS—UNIQUE AND REFRESHING

I love petunias in planters. They are a classic annual flower well suited for hanging baskets and containers. Originally from South America, this flower of vibrant colors loves full sun. With bigger flowers than the popular Million Bells® (*Calibrachoa*), petunias attract attention and work well in combination with other flowers in a planter. They are tender perennials in USDA hardiness zones 9–11.

Yellow has traditionally been an elusive color for petunias, but this is changing. One of my favorites is Supertunia® 'Citrus' Petunia. It has a dark yellow center with a light yellow to white edging, which makes for a striking flower. The creamy yellow looks good with anything, but it's especially exciting when paired with blue or purple flowers. Supertunia® has large blossoms that attract butterflies and hummingbirds. They are vigorous bloomers but they require full sun, water, and frequent feeding to stay at their peak. When you plant it in a container in spring, incorporate a slow-release fertilizer suitable for flowers into the potting soil and follow up through the growing season with liquid fertilizer.

Petunia Cascadias™ 'Indian Summer' is also outstanding. The large, lightly ruffled blossoms are a distinctive mix of yellow, orange, and salmon pink, unrivaled in petunias. They bloom profusely from early spring until first frost and withstand the summer heat well. It has a trailing, well-branched habit so it spills out over the edge of a container beautifully. Its height is 10 to 12 inches with a spread of 12 to 14 inches wide.

In a white window box, the large blossoms of Cascadias™ 'Indian Summer' petunias blend with deep pink petunias to create an eye-catching summer show.

Left: The glorious Supertunia® 'Citrus' Petunia (*Petunia* Supertunia® 'Citrus') is planted in an appealing fluted urn. Its buttery-yellow blooms grow here with tall, purple angelonia and 'Sweet Caroline Sweetheart Lime' sweet potato vine (*Ipomoea hybrid*). Petunia Supertunia® needs no deadheading. These petunias grow as somewhat trailing plants. It can be a perennial in zones 9–11. In zones 3–8 it is an annual.

Right: In a black container, the yellow Supertunia® 'Citrus' Petunia (*Petunia* Supertunia® 'Citrus') joins the trailing white fan flower (*Scaevola aemula*). The black and yellow combo is a dramatic touch. Perfect for modern landscapes.

9. WINDOW BOX INSPIRATION

Window boxes are coming back in style! They dress up a window and offer a gardener yet another place to grow flowers. They also brighten up a streetscape or a home's façade with happy flowers and greenery. Having a window box is one of the most neighborly things you can do in the warmer months of the year.

In the early 20th century in the United States, window boxes were at their peak of popularity. Houses were being built on smaller lots, with many close to the street, and historical styles such as cozy English cottages and inviting Dutch colonials were in vogue. Window boxes were a per-

fect match. They also fit the 1920s Spanish and Mediterranean–style houses. The popularity of window boxes faded as suburban homes and large lawns became the norm.

Today, we are embracing apartment and town-home living. The smaller lots and patios have us looking again to window boxes (and modern deck-railing planters) to satisfy our thirst for gardening. For example, why not grow a small kitchen garden in a planter box hung outside a window? Imagine opening the window and harvesting some lettuce or nasturtiums to dress up a salad?

The considerations of proportion and scale are important when it comes to window boxes. A well-proportioned window box has an appealing look, but one that is too small looks silly. As for length, the box should extend several inches beyond the windowsill or shutters, if you have them. As far as width, I suggest extra-large window boxes that are wider and deeper than usual. How wide and deep is a matter of proportions, which is all in the eye of the beholder. A good rule of thumb is that the height of the window box should be 20 to 25 percent of the height of your window. If you use large brackets to support your flower boxes, add their dimensions to your calculations.

Top: I recommend using large window boxes if you want a flowerful display such as this one. Big window boxes can hold more soil and won't dry out as quickly as smaller ones, allowing you to plant fewer drought-tolerant plants. Here, flowers and foliage were planted together, including the versatile lime-green sweet potato vine (*Ipomoea batatas*).

Bottom: This deep window box drops into a black metal holder, which is visible beneath the flowers. Metal supports are a decorative and sturdy solution to supporting the weight of long window boxes. The trailing flower is 'New Gold' lantana, a heat-loving perennial (annual in northern regions) that blooms from spring to fall—excellent for tumbling from planters and hanging baskets.

10. THE ART OF WATERING PLANTERS

Planters and pots dry out more quickly than the soil in the ground. This means you must water your planters more often than planting beds, especially in hot, sunny weather. Larger pots contain more soil and retain water better than smaller pots. As a result, larger pots retain more water than smaller pots. This is helpful because then you do not need to water as much, and you will tend not to overwater. The most common cause of plant death in containers is overwatering. We kill our plants with watering kindness.

So how to know when to water a pot? Before watering, check to see if the soil is moist. Stick your finger into the soil to about the second knuckle. If it feels dry below your knuckle, water it until water comes out of the drainage hole in the bottom of the pot. Water thoroughly to encourage the plant roots to follow the water down into the lower half of the pot. Deeper roots mean you won't have to water as often.

The time of year affects watering frequency. In spring, when the plants are small and the temperatures are cool, you will not have to water often. In summer, when the sun is strong, the plants are large, and the temperatures are higher, you may have to water daily. It all depends on the size of the planter, which plants are growing, and your climate.

I recommend using a watering wand with a so-called water breaker attached. This kind of head has a lot of tiny holes that generate a light spray. The fine spray will not damage tender flowering plants. I also suggest using a wand with a built-in shutoff valve in the handle. This allows you to conserve water and adjust the flow.

And lastly, it is best not to water at night. If you water your plants too late in the day the foliage will not dry and this will encourage disease to develop. Water in the morning, if possible; then the plants will have all day to absorb it.

Left: Look for a garden hose that is durable and resists kinking. Store hoses coiled up. A hose pot, as shown, has an interior guide that lets you wind a hose around it without tangling. Before you buy, determine the length you need. A large diameter hose will provide the most water, faster. The three basic hose diameters are ½ inch, ⅝ inch, and ¾ inch. The largest diameter hose delivers up to 25 gallons per minute.

Right: Hanging hoses can be cumbersome, but this is a neat solution that uses a metal grid as a backing. If watering planters becomes a chore, or if you go away often, consider installing a drip irrigation system.

11. SAME POT, SAME PLACE—DIFFERENT COLOR

One of the joys of growing flowers in large planters is that you can change the display every year or even every season. Once you find a type of flower that thrives in your particular conditions, you may want to keep planting it every year in the same planter. But why not experiment with the available colors of that specific plant? For example, if you find that the lovely upright summer snapdragon (*Angelonia*) does well in a large pot outside your door, you can plant purple angelonia one year, such as 'Angelface Purple,' and switch to a raspberry-pink variety the next, such as 'Serenita Raspberry.'

I did that with New Guinea impatiens (*Impatiens hawkeri*), a hybrid form of impatiens. I suggested these low-maintenance plants to a client because they are super easy annual flowers that can be used alone or in combination to fill eye-popping planters. They tolerate more sun than traditional shade-loving impatiens and have larger blooms. And they come in a range of dazzling colors, including orange, red, pink, white, purple, and lavender. Best of all, New Guinea impatiens are highly resistant to downy mildew that afflicts traditional impatiens.

In two planters flanking a stately wood bench (shown in photo), we planted deep red New Guinea impatiens. The planters were filled with blooms all summer into fall. The next year we stayed with our choice of New Guinea impatiens but changed the color to a softer orange-tinged pink. The effect was just as floriferous and striking.

This highlights how exciting the annual flower world has become. Every year breeders introduce new series or cultivars of our favorite flowers, featuring new colors, patterns, and growth habits. For example, New Guinea impatiens now come in almost fluorescent colors and bicolor forms. You can also find them with two-toned, and even three-toned, foliage that is just as beautiful as the flowers. There are so many choices! I guess it calls for more planters in your garden . . .

Top: New Guinea impatiens have abundant blooms that keep going all summer into fall. They grow in part sun to part shade. Fun fact: The original plants were found on a plant expedition to New Guinea in 1970. The botanists saw the magnificent impatiens growing wild and brought them back to the United States. Hybrid crosses made with other *Impatiens* species from Java and the Celebes Islands resulted in the New Guinea impatiens that are grown today.

Bottom, left: The unique orange-pink extra-large flowers of Sonic® 'Mango' New Guinea impatiens light up a shady corner. This is a compact plant that works well in a planter. They like water and will wilt dramatically if allowed to dry out.

Bottom, right: A close-up view of Sonic® 'Mango' New Guinea impatiens highlights the thick five-petaled flowers with orange and darker pink markings. The other flower colors in the compact Sonic series include Magic Pink, Deep Purple, and Amethyst, among others.

12. THRILLER-FILLER-SPILLER

A successful way to pot up flowering containers is to use the thriller-filler-spiller technique. This design approach uses three different types of plants to create a tiered, full display. The central thriller plant, in the middle of the pot, is the focal point. It is the tallest plant and adds a vertical element to the mix. It provides the drama. The thriller can be a flowering or foliage plant, or even an ornamental grass such as purple fountain grass. Plant this one up first in the planter. The next are the filler plants. They surround the thriller and add a rounded appearance to the pot. For this reason, choose plants that have a mounded growth habit. You can use several different plants and interplant them around the thriller. I like to use foliage and annual flowers for this. A few annuals to consider include Diamond Frost® euphorbia, petunia, heliotrope, and lantana.

The last to be planted are the spillers. These are trailing plants that hang over the edge of the planter. These spread and soften the look of the planter. They can also unify the planting if you choose flowers that echo the colors of the other plants. Or you can use trailing plants with unusual textured leaves to add interest to the overall scheme. Some examples are trailing bacopa (*Sutera cordata*), sweet potato vine, golden creeping Jenny, licorice plant, and variegated ivy.

The thriller-filler-spiller technique is a surefire way to create gorgeous planters. You can vary the height of the central thriller and use tall canna lilies to dominate the scene. Or you can go for the shorter angelonia that almost blends in with the rest.

A tall Lily of the Nile, 'Glen Avon' (*Agapanthus praecox* 'Glen Avon') steals the show as the thriller in this outstanding planter. Its sturdy stems hold rounded flower heads consisting of pale blue flowers with a violet stripe along each petal. It is a perennial in zones 8–11. Blooms from July to September. Below it is the filler plant, Diamond Frost® euphorbia. A purple calibrachoa and yellow creeping Jenny (*Lysimachia nummularia* 'Aurea') are the glorious spiller plants. Created by Michael's Garden Gate Nursery, Mount Kisco, New York.

Left: The upright habit of growth of 'Serena Lavender' angelonia (known also as summer snapdragon) makes it perfect as the center thriller in this low-growing thriller-filler-spiller container combination. It has beautiful spikes of 16 inches tall, lavender pea-like flowers with dark eyes from late spring to late summer. Needs sun. It is surrounded by petunias, calibrachoas, and the bicolor blooms of 'BeBop Pink' verbena. By Michael's Garden Gate Nursery, Mount Kisco, New York.

Right: A striking, tall princess flower (*Tibouchina urvilleana*) adds a tropical touch to a planter. It is an evergreen shrub that is hardy in zones 10–11, so many gardeners use this as an annual (unless they can take it indoors to overwinter). The deep purple flowers bloom throughout summer in partial to full sun. The filler and spillers are annual flowers—white Diamond Frost® euphorbia and blue 'Crystal Palace' lobelia. By Michael's Garden Gate Nursery, Mount Kisco, New York.

13. CONSIDER A POTTING TABLE

Once you embark on creating planters full of foliage and flowers, you may soon tire of bending over to fill pots and plant them up. A raised work area, otherwise known as a potting table or potting bench, may be in your future. It is a handy place for starting seeds, storing small tools, or potting up planters. Once you have one you will wonder how you ever did without it.

If you are handy, you can make a potting table out of wood. An informative website for building a DIY potting bench is on *This Old House* (www .thisoldhouse.com/how-to/how-to-build-potting -bench). You can, of course, purchase a potting bench or table. There are many on the market, and you'll undoubtedly find one that fits your budget. A potting table does not have to be cumbersome. You can purchase a ready-made one that is constructed from lightweight metal, or you could even repurpose a rolling metal or composite utility cart.

Consider where you will locate the table before you make or buy one. Determine the length and the width that will fit your spot. Be sure to locate the potting bench near an outdoor water source. Here are a few more considerations:

- The potting table should be sturdy and be made of rot-resistant material.
- It should have a strong shelf to hold pots, watering cans, and other supplies.
- If the table is not under a roof then the surface must be able to withstand the weather. The tabletop can be galvanized steel or some other smooth surface.
- Strong hooks on the sides are handy for hanging tools and towels.
- A backboard adds more surface area for hanging tools.

Indoor or outdoor potting benches are a boon to a gardener. They can be placed anywhere—this workstation is partially dug into the earth, so the back of the table is level with the ground. A great way to hide the service area! This potting table is covered with plastic so that water and fertilizer do not harm its surface.

14. BIDENS—A SUN LOVER

Bidens (*Bidens ferulifolia*) is a little-known plant with yellow or orange daisy-like flowers. This short, spreading perennial with deeply divided, bright green foliage was originally found growing in southern Arizona and Mexico. It has since been bred into several large-flowered cultivars that are used as sun-loving annuals in cooler climate gardens. Bidens tolerates dry conditions when established and is well suited for planters and hanging baskets.

The beauty of Bidens is in its copious flowers and unique foliage. In fact, its species name, *ferulifolia*, refers to its ferny, fennel-like leaves. I like the Bidens cultivar known as Goldilocks Rocks®, which is a compact, trailing variety developed by Proven Winners. It grows 6 to 10 inches in height and has a 10- to 14- inches spread. It sports large, golden-yellow flowers along its cascading stems. The flowers are up to 3 inches across. Goldilocks Rocks® blooms from late spring to the end of fall, tolerates high heat, is drought tolerant, and is continuous blooming. Best of all, no deadheading of spent blossoms is required. It is a great spiller flower for combining with others in a planter. You can grow it as a perennial in USDA hardiness zones 9–11.

Proven Winners, a leading consumer plant brand and top-notch online source for flower information, classifies Bidens as a "second to go out" plant. This means you do not take your plant outside too early in the spring. Bidens does not like the cold. Wait until all danger of frost has passed. It requires a sunny location and well-drained soil. Good drainage is essential for Bidens. Provide drainage holes in your planter, use a quality potting mix, and elevate your planter with pot feet or something similar.

Top: I combined Goldilocks Rocks® Bidens (*Bidens ferulifolia*) with purple ornamental cabbage and orange ornamental peppers in this fall planter. The bright yellow flowers insert a happy pop, and the bright green foliage sets it off nicely. I trimmed back the Bidens to keep it well shaped.

Bottom: A close-up of Goldilocks Rocks® Bidens showing happy flowers and fernlike foliage.

Top, left: The snowy-white blooms of 'Whirlwind White' fan flower, an annual, is a perfect choice for sunny planters, raised beds, and hanging baskets. It has a low, prostrate growth habit and can be grown alone or in combination with others in a container. Fan flower is self-cleaning, so no deadheading is necessary.

Top, right: The ice cream colors of 'Blue Wonder' fan flower and 'Bandana Pink' lantana blend beautifully as they spill over the rim of an outdoor planter. Both of these flowers are tender perennials but are grown as deer-resistant annuals in cooler climates. They do exceptionally well in the heat of summer.

Left: The yellow bamboo-like blades of 'All Gold' Japanese forest grass (*Hakonechloa macra* 'All Gold') create an eye-catching contrast to the profuse flowers of Whirlwind White fan flower (*Scaevola aemula* 'Whirlwind White'). This graceful low-growing ornamental grass holds its bright golden color and makes an excellent companion to any of the colorful spreading blooms of fan flower. It is a wonderful deer-resistant combination for planters.

15. THE WONDROUS FAN FLOWER— GREAT IN PLANTERS

What is that flower? Many people ask about the unusual semi-tropical Australian fan flower, whose botanical name is *Scaevola* (skay-VO-lah) *aemula*. It spreads out happily from a container and is unlike any other flower in that it displays its petals in a 1-inch-wide, fanlike arrangement on one side of the stem. The fan of petals resembles a left hand with five fingers, giving it the Latin name, *Scaevola*, which means left hand. In Hawaii, the related native plant, *Scaevola taccada*, is called naupaka. According to legend, a Hawaiian princess tore the flower in half after being banned from marrying her commoner lover. The flowers mourned to see the young lovers' hearts broken. As a memorial to their love, when the naupaka flower blooms, it only blooms in halves.

Fan flower is a tender perennial in USDA hardiness zones 10–11 but is best grown as an annual flower in hanging baskets and containers. It makes a great spiller due to its cascading branches that are festooned with a nonstop show of blue, pink, or white flowers. This heat- and humidity-tolerant flower grows 8 to 12 inches tall and its trailing form flows over a container's edge. Plant in full to part sun in well-drained soil and water regularly. Fan flower is drought tolerant and produces a constant bloom throughout the heat of summer to first frost. It is an easy-care flower, and deadheading is not necessary. It is deer and rabbit resistant.

There are several cultivars of fan flower available, including the popular 'Blue Wonder.' New cultivars include smaller, more compact plants or different colors of flowers. These include 'Whirlwind Blue' fan flower, which has violet-blue flowers and grows 10 inches tall with twice as much spread; and Scampi Pink fan flower, which grows just 6 inches tall and is 24 inches wide.

16. THE ENDURING POPULARITY OF BLUE PLANTERS

Blue, blue, we all love blue. Could this be why blue planters continue to be so popular? Today's consumers do indeed gravitate toward planters with natural, neutral shades and basic colors like black, white, and gray. But retailers have found that cobalt blue planters are standing the test of time and are still being sought out by planter lovers. It may be because blue is America's favorite color. We love blue flowers and blue Crayola crayons. In fact, Classic Blue was the 2020 Pantone Color of the Year. We cannot get enough blue in our lives.

It's no wonder, then, that there is such a great variety of blue containers available. The most common is the glazed cobalt blue planter. Anything that is planted in this deep, rich color seems to pop. But before you buy a ceramic planter, you should determine if it is a quality product. The only way to know is to ask and find out how the pot was made. Glazed ceramic pots can be waterproof and frost proof, provided the clay is fired at a high enough heat. The ceramic glaze that provides the color also affects the pot's durability. You do not want cracks, and you won't want the color to fade in the sun. Many ceramic pots cannot stay outside in very cold winter weather. Also make sure the planter comes with one or more drainage holes. This is essential.

Large, deep-blue glazed pots, unquestionably, are eye-catching. They make a stylish statement wherever they are placed. The combination of blue with green foliage is a soothing visual treat for the eyes, and it adds instant color to a deck or balcony. They can flank a front door, sit at the corner of a terrace, or even be placed within a plant bed.

Top, left: Tall blue planters add a splash of enduring color to a patio or deck. Matching ones double the fun, as shown here. My friend, Joanne Goldstein, combined delicate blue lobelia and orange-toned *Diascia*, or twinspur.

Top, right: An early spring planting in a cobalt-blue planter. The planting mix includes pansies, Johnny-jump-ups (*Viola*), white sweet alyssum (*Lobularia maritima*), and yellow Nemesia (*Nemesia strumosa*). By Michael's Garden Gate Nursery, Mount Kisco, New York.

Bottom, left: A shiny, textured blue-glazed urn makes quite a statement next to green plants in the garden. No flowers necessary.

Bottom, right: This blue pot is placed atop pot feet. This allows water to drain out of the pot—very important. The flowers greet visitors as they enter. *Photo by Laura Hendrix McKillop.*

17. OVER THE EDGE—GREAT SPILLERS TO USE

Spiller plants, which trail over the side of a container, finish off a planter in a professional-looking way. They soften the edges and create contrast with the pot beneath. Containers of upright flowers can be made more interesting with the addition of a spiller plant or two. It is just as important as the prominent center plant. Foliage plants—plants with no flowers—make great spillers. I like to use three different foliage plants as spillers.

'Silver Falls' dichondra (*Dichondra argentea* 'Silver Falls') is a spectacular spiller plant for baskets and containers. It has small, fan-shaped silver leaves on thin silver stems, and it is very heat and drought tolerant. The leaves can easily trail 3 to 6 feet over a hanging basket or container. It creates a dramatic scene when it sways in the breeze. If the stems get too long, simply snip them. Grow as an annual; it is hardy in USDA hardiness zones 10–12.

A very effective spiller is the golden creeping Jenny (*Lysimachia nummularia* 'Aurea'). It has yellow flowers in summer but its golden hanging foliage is the show. Creeping Jenny will cascade over the edge and form dense strands of leaves that hang straight down. It thrives in sun or shade, though it retains its yellow color in the sun. There is one drawback: creeping Jenny is considered to be an invasive plant. This vine should be restricted to planters only, and it cannot be sold or shipped to certain states due to this status. It is suitable for USDA hardiness zones 4–8.

Vinca vine is a widely used spiller plant. I especially like the variegated 'Wojo's Gem' vinca vine. Its leaves have large, yellow-white centers edged with deep green. It is hardy in USDA hardiness zones 7–9; north of zone 7 it is used as an annual. I also like the dark green, cold-hardy myrtle (*Vinca minor*). It is normally used as an evergreen ground cover, but its trailing habit makes myrtle a resilient spiller in containers, especially in cooler weather.

Top: The silver-gray foliage of 'Silver Falls' dichondra (*Dichondra argentea* 'Silver Falls') spills exuberantly over a rustic wooden window box. The metallic gray foliage contrasts nicely with the large, deep green leaves and pink blooms of hybrid begonias.

Bottom, left: Tall, slender planters like this one are perfect for the long, luxuriant yellow-leaved strands of creeping Jenny (*Lysimachia nummularia* 'Aurea').

Bottom, right: Myrtle (*Vinca minor*) is a tough, reliable trailing plant most often used as a ground cover. It offers evergreen foliage and blue spring flowers. Varieties include blue, white, or wine-purple flowers. Its dark green leaves look great when hanging over a white pot beneath brightly colored zinnias, as shown here.

18. THE JOY OF SPRINGTIME PLANTERS

After a long, dark Northeastern winter, I long to see some outdoor color. As the drab gray world slowly brightens, thoughts of early spring colorful blossoms crowd out everything else. That is when I fill a few planters with fresh potting mix and plant up cold-hardy spring flowers in pastel colors. I cannot wait for seeds to sprout or cuttings to root, so I buy small flowering plants and plant them up as soon as the danger of hard frost has passed. The dose of bright colors that spring flowers offer is "just what the doctor ordered" and portend the promise of a new garden.

The key to success for spring planters is to use annual and perennial flowers that flourish in cool weather. Good choices include petunias, tulips, coral bells, bleeding heart, and sweet alyssum. I recommend that you wait until nighttime temperatures are consistently above freezing before planting outside. For example, petunias can tolerate a nighttime temperature of about 39 degrees but are damaged at 32 degrees. Below-freezing temperatures will kill the plant. If a light frost threatens, you might cover the planter and plants with a sheet. And keep a plant's sun and shade preferences in mind. This is especially important in spring when the sun's rays are not that strong. While petunias will grow in a partially shaded location, they will have a more abundant bloom in a sunny spot. Check the plant label for sun and/or shade requirements.

Spring planters seem to make a bigger impression than planters full of flowers later in the year. I suppose this is only natural, as the appearance of vibrant flowers is such a welcome change to our color-starved eyes. As Gertrude S. Wister, a 20th-century horticulturist and author, noted, "The flowers of late winter and early spring occupy places in our hearts well out of proportion to their size."

Top, left: Every year, in early spring, I plant a blue columbine in a planter by my front door. Here is the hybrid 'Swan Blue and White' columbine (*Aquilegia × hybrida* 'Swan Blue and White'), which has fine, long spurs and large bicolor blossoms held atop sturdy 24-inch stems. It is a deer-resistant, spring-blooming perennial. After the flowers have passed in summer, I lift it and plant it in a flower bed. Excellent for cutting. Zones 3–8.

Top, right: Celebrate spring! I created this wide entry landing for a client and located a bench there. She promptly made it a welcoming entrance by placing her collection of planters all around and filling them with bright yellow tulips, pansies, trailing white bacopa, and more. Spring flowers, however short-lived, make all the difference.

Bottom, left: Pink and white flowers make a delightful spring planter. Here, snowy sweet alyssum (*Lobularia maritima*), a reliable annual, joins verbena, a pink, early flowering annual. Perennial coral bells (*Heuchera*) sends its dainty, dark pink flower skyward. Wait for all danger of frost to pass before setting out this planter combination. By Michael's Garden Gate Nursery, Mount Kisco, New York.

Bottom, right: A close-up of the snowy blooms of sweet alyssum. New varieties of fragrant sweet alyssum, such as 'Snow Princess' and 'White Knight,' have enhanced heat tolerance and vigor.

The pot feet under this planter are hardly noticeable, especially when the hybrid I'Conia Begonia 'Unbelievable Lucky Strike' is in bloom. This mounding plant does not stop blooming until the first hard frost! It thrives in part shade. I interplanted it with the airy white euphorbia Diamond Frost® and 'FlameThrower' coleus (peeking out the back).

19. POT FEET—A USEFUL AND FUN ACCESSORY

Planters need drainage. This is a rule you cannot forget, otherwise the potting soil gets waterlogged and plants literally drown. Well-drained potting soil makes all the difference in growing healthy plants in your planters! I have learned this from direct experience. So drainage holes in the base of any planter is vitally important. But the other equally important thing is to make sure that water can flow freely out of the planter. You can do this by lifting the pot slightly off the surface where it rests. To do this, you can use small, flat, weatherproof items like pebbles or a flat stone or brick. Or you can buy what is commonly referred to as pot risers, pot feet, or pot toes. They are handy accessories.

Pot feet raise a planter evenly off the ground and keep your plants "high and dry" by allowing water to drain and air to circulate under the pot. Best of all, your planter will not leave any unsightly stains under its base. This can be helpful on wood decks, concrete patios, and stone landings.

Pot feet can be visible or unseen. It depends on the look you prefer. Visible pot feet sit like small pedestal holders around the perimeter of a planter's base. Three or four uniform pot feet are required for a large planter, and their appearance can be admired by all. Unseen pot risers look like small dark rings or hockey pucks. They are made from hard rubber or plastic and sit underneath the center of the planter, which make the pot look like it is floating. This is a subtle effect that works well with modern-style containers.

The shapes of visible pot feet are where the fun happens! You can get terracotta or stone pot feet in decorative styles that match your planter.

You can even buy them in the shape of cats, birds, frogs, and more. If you want to color coordinate a glazed planter, matching pot feet are available as well.

Four pot feet under a large ornate planter make it seem like it's on a low pedestal. The water drains from the pot and goes directly into the drain grate in the corner.

20. THE MANY FACES OF METAL PLANTERS

Metal planters have a long history. The Greeks and Romans fashioned copper into planters, and 19th-century European estates used zinc to make troughs and pots. Both materials, with their extraordinary patinated finishes, are still popular today. Copper develops a rich verdigris finish, and zinc, when weathered, features a light gray mottled patina. I especially like zinc planters for their vintage look. They are also lightweight, a plus for balconies and terraces.

An alternative to historic zinc pots are modern steel planters with a galvanized zinc coating. The strength of the steel combines with the weather protection of a zinc coating, which is perfect for larger planters where rigidity is important.

The appeal of contemporary styling has fueled the popularity of metal planters, particularly those made from Corten steel. This type of steel, when exposed to weather, develops a layer of protective rust that has an attractive brown-red patina. The surface rust will never eat through the metal. This is one of Corten's biggest benefits in the landscape.

The primary drawback to all metal planters is the fact that they are prone to overheating, which can damage plant roots. Manufacturers of metal planters often provide Styrofoam insulation inside the planter to buffer the temperature and ensure that plants stay healthy in both hot and cold climates. Another drawback for metal planters is the potential for excessive rusting in areas with a lot of rainfall or humid subtropic weather. For this reason, manufacturers recommend that metal planters that are prone to rust be kept under a roof or in a sheltered location.

A tall, tapered metal planter crafted from Corten steel sits in a covered entryway. The simple and modern style, combined with the rusted patina, fits a minimalist scheme well.

Here, a wire basket containing pink-and-yellow lantana and purple fan flower (*Scaevola*) was placed within an antique metal urn. Simply remove the basket from the urn when watering the plants.

Above: A large cast-stone planter lights up a corner. It is filled with white chrysanthemums surrounded by the white strappy leaves of 'Evergold' sedge (*Carex oshimensis* 'Evergold') and blue calibrachoa. The white flowers glow at night.

Left: Rich magenta chrysanthemums illustrate the power of one color. Three planters filled with the same flowers make a striking statement.

21. PLANTERS FOR FALL

When the cooler weather and shorter days of early fall arrive, summer planters may look a bit bedraggled. Sometimes I keep them going until the tender plants succumb to the cold, but often I simply replace the summer display with fall flowers. I love the flowers of autumn and delight in the deeper, richer colors that the cool weather brings out. Fall planters filled with eye-popping blooms, grasses, and even succulents celebrate the season in a quietly jubilant fashion.

Of course, the queen of fall flowers for planters are chrysanthemums. They are unquestionably one of our most popular flowers, and few plants can rival their beautiful colors and durability. They bloom for a long period, make excellent cut flowers, and are easy to grow in containers. Plant them singly in a planter or mix them with other plants—it is your choice. I personally like fall mums filling a planter by themselves. I particularly like white ones because they glow brightly in the darkness of a fall evening. They seem to light up under a full moon.

Another popular flower for fall planters are pansies. Long associated with spring, the cold-tolerant hybrids of this happy-faced perennial bloom in fall and can even overwinter in USDA hardiness zones 6 and 7. So, along with mums, add pansies in fall containers. And don't forget asters, sedums, and goldenrod. Goldenrod (*Solidago*) is a perennial that blooms in late summer to fall. It can be grown easily in containers and mixes well with ornamental grasses and decorative cabbage and kale. And why not pop in a few ornamental peppers with their colorful fruits and foliage? All these together make a notable fall planter display.

Yellow pansies share the stage with the red fruits and dark green leaves of wintergreen (*Gaultheria procumbens*). Place a few unique winged gourds within the planter for a festive fall look. The dark green boxwood makes a good backdrop.

22. THE NEW VERBENAS

If you want a butterfly and hummingbird magnet that also creates a stunning summer show in your containers, then try one of the enchanting verbenas. These vintage flowers have been grown for generations, but they were known for being fussy and prone to disease. That has changed with the improved, modern verbena hybrids (*Verbena × hybrida*), commonly known as garden verbena.

The hybrid cultivars are short-lived tender perennials (USDA hardiness zones 9–10) and are grown as annuals in northern climates. Their long-blooming flowers rise above fernlike foliage and bloom from May to October. The tiny flowers form rounded clusters that come in shades of blue-violet, purple, rose, red, pink, coral, and white, as well as bicolored varieties. They also may have white eyes, stripes, fringed petals, and more. Verbena is a winner when growing in a planter.

You can find hybrid verbenas that trail or others that grow somewhat upright to 18 inches tall. They make lovely fillers or spillers in planters. Consistent watering and a very sunny spot is important. The secret to great hybrid verbenas in containers is to pinch them back to promote bushier growth. Do not be afraid to cut them back! Deadheading faded flowers also encourages additional blooms. Some hybrid verbenas, such as the wonderful Superbena®, do not need to be deadheaded.

Verbenas pair well with other flowers. Plant two different colors of hybrid verbenas with angelonia, Bidens, calibrachoa, and creeping Jenny for a floriferous planter. Or try the fabulous bicolored verbenas. Hybrid verbenas with their colors and patterns are wonderful eye candy.

Above: I planted this lovely pink verbena in a basket-weave terracotta pot and placed it in a bed. The tawny red coral bells (*Heuchera*) foliage accent the flowers and pot perfectly.

Opposite page: 'BeBop Pink' verbena, with its two-tone pink rounded flowers, trails over the edge of a pot, along with a similar lavender white-eyed verbena. Unique flower patterns are a feature of hybrid verbenas. They are both mounding and trailing—great for containers.

23. ELEVATE THAT PLANTER

Planters filled with flowers inject color and grace to any outdoor setting. An effective display technique is elevating the planter to make it more noticeable. My favorite planter locations are atop walls, on steps, or set high on a stand or pedestal. The idea is to raise the pot off the ground—sitting on anything—to show it off.

This is not a new idea. In the 19th century, Victorians displayed their potted plants aloft in lightweight, decorative wire stands. This style has reemerged today with both vintage wire plant stands and the popular modern metal planter holders. The variety of stand styles is tremendous, ranging from whimsical to sleek.

An easy way to elevate planters is to set them on posts, walls, or steps. I especially like placing pots on a series of outdoor steps for the graduated look of "pot upon pot." They don't have to match. In fact, the more varied it is, the more eclectic and fun it all looks. A design tip: don't place a planter that is too big or too small on a wall. If the pot is out of scale to the base that it sits on, it looks awkward. Also keep the styles consistent—a modern planter on a contemporary plant stand works well, but an old-fashioned urn looks odd in the same stand.

There are some great repurposing ideas for plant stands that you might try. For years I used a terracotta flue pipe as a plant stand, set within a plant bed. I got it at a stone supply yard. I placed a 1½-inch-thick bluestone paver on top of the flue pipe, then I set a pot on the flat paver. You can also use large flat rocks, tree stumps, and upside-down pots as planter bases. Other possibilities for displaying smaller pots of flowers include ladders propped up at an angle against a wall, old step stools, and even old chairs that are maybe a little moss covered. I am sure I have forgotten some other neat ideas, but you get the point: elevate it!

Top, left: A Victorian-style welded wire plant stand, complete with decorative twisted curlicues, withstands the elements and is part of a summer garden. Note the wooden boards that act as a strong base for the heavy planters. They are a helpful added support to the lightweight wire shelf.

Top, right: An antique, moss-covered pedestal (see the monkey?) serves as a convenient base for an ornate metal urn filled with white New Guinea impatiens. It is a sweet surprise, placed in a partially shady plant bed.

Bottom: I placed three small pots of flowers on three consecutive stone steps. The contrast of the pink calibrachoa and white trailing ornamental bacopa (*Sutera cordata*) against the stone is very appealing. Watering daily is a must because the planters are small.

> "Making a garden is not a gentle hobby for the elderly, to be picked up and laid down like a game of solitaire. It is a grand passion. It seizes a person whole, and once it has done so he will have to accept that his life is going to be radically changed."
> —MAY SARTON, *PLANT DREAMING DEEP*

FLOWER GARDEN PLANTING TIPS

Gardening—especially with flowering plants such as annuals and perennials—can become a grand passion, as the 20th-century American writer May Sarton noted. Working with Nature to show off her floral creations is a delightfully satisfying task that can "seize a person whole." If you think about it, planting a flower garden is similar to creating a painting or a ceramic piece except that, besides indulging our creative instincts, we must abide by Nature's whims. If it gets too hot, our flowers may suffer from thirst; and if it gets too cold, they may freeze. The pests may invite themselves in, or mildew may inflict itself upon the leaves.

Despite this fact of life, we gardeners persist. Why? Because gardening engages our senses and connects us to the undulating rhythms of the natural world. We enjoy the flow. And this enjoyment makes us optimists. We are always looking forward to the next growing season when we can plant our white-themed "moonlight garden" or tend our perennial pollinator landscape. The call of a spring morning inspires us to get out the shovel and the hose, and to turn the soil to make room for yet another flowering plant that we *absolutely* must have. Optimism prevails, even though we know it is an iffy proposition. You cannot expect success every time. As Sarton said, "Making a garden is not a gentle hobby."

This chapter, Flower Garden Planting Tips, is intended to aid you in creating a new flower garden or enhancing one you already have. I emphasize practicality and following Nature's lead. The gardening tips in this chapter are meant to provide you with hands-on techniques for turning over soil and caring for successful flower beds. It is not a comprehensive how-to manual but a compilation of some choice pointers I have learned and used over the decades to create gardens for myself and others (my company website is www.johnsenlandscapes.com). These tips make it easier to garden or at least make it more fun to work outdoors. I hope the suggestions and the photos I share will have you itching to go out and get your hands dirty.

Above: A green-and-white flower! 'Spring Green' viridiflora tulip is white with a delicate band of pale green down the outside of each petal. They develop their best color in semi-shade and have strong, straight stems and grow 12 to 24 inches tall. Viridiflora tulips bloom in early to late May and last up to three weeks. Plant bulbs in fall for spring display. Zones 3–7.

Left: Hybrid begonias, blue lobelia, and bicolor pink New Guinea impatiens make this part-sun flower bed a knockout.

24. FLOWER GARDENING TIPS—WHY BOTHER?

When I was in college years ago, I studied landscape architecture at the University of Hawaii and lived on an organic farm. They were two distinctly different worlds, and I was pulled in both directions. In class, I learned about design styles, theory, materials, and functional requirements. On our working farm, I amended the soil, planted crops, and dealt with pests and wildlife. It was theory versus practice, and neither side seemed to recognize the other. Michael Pollan, the author and journalist, described the situation well when he wrote in the *New York Times Book Review* magazine in 1991: "I was perplexed at how few of the more literary garden books bothered to talk about so basic a gardening operation as digging, or even planting—there was little about the processes of gardening. . . . Everybody seemed to jump right from wintertime sketches and plans to the glorious blooms of July."

Luckily, times have changed. Now our attention goes to the soil and native plants as much as to design and layout. It's a combination that allows you to create a striking landscape and feed pollinators at the same time. In fact, this "hands in the dirt" mindset is almost a rule for all great garden-making and design endeavors. For flower gardening it starts with a Nature-based approach. If you know about a flower's likes and dislikes, the soil and climate it prefers, and how to plant it properly, you are on the road to success.

Why bother with all this? Because flower gardening is one way to bond with Nature and slow down your busy life. You become more observant of Nature's processes and, in so doing, become part of it yourself. And the more you know, the more you can enjoy the menial tasks that are required. Soon you will discover that your hard work will be rewarded. Nature will pay you back handsomely—in flowers! What a great way to begin, or continue on, your gardening journey.

Above: Sturdy tools help make gardening enjoyable. Buy top-quality tools that will last a long time. It makes all the difference! Use your foot to exert power on a spade. This is important to making a clean plant bed edge, as shown here. Insert straight down. A spade works better than a half-moon edger, which does not dig deep enough to create a suitable edge. The shovel or spade should be kept sharp to make it easy to cut through soil and plant matter.

Opposite page: North American native Gloriosa daisies (*Rudbeckia hirta*) are a short-lived perennial related to black-eyed Susans. They are a lovely wildflower with yellow blooms and a touch of rust in the dark center. Gloriosa daisies bloom in late mid- to late summer; they love the sun. They often seed themselves. Gloriosa daisies grow to be 12 to 36 inches tall. Zones 3–8. *Photo by Laura Hendrix McKillop.*

Above: Tutti Frutti 'Apricot Delight' yarrow (*Achillea millefolium* 'Apricot Delight') is a tough perennial that loves sun and stands up to heat and humidity. A fast grower, it reaches 18 to 22 inches tall and wide. It tolerates dry soils. This perennial's showy, umbel flower clusters of apricot, pink, and deep rose bloom from summer into fall. The foliage is soft and fernlike. Yarrow attracts butterflies to the garden and is deer and rabbit resistant. Zones 3–9.

Left: The deep orange-and-yellow blossoms of the annual 'Luscious Citrus Blend' lantana blend with French marigold 'Safari Yellow.' The silvery leaves of dusty miller add contrast. All are suited to high temperatures and hot sun. Deer resistant.

25. HOT WEATHER FLOWER GARDEN TIPS

Hot weather can strain our passion for flower gardening. Both the flowers and the gardener may start to look stressed and bedraggled in the heat. But you can have a flower garden that thrives in a hot, sunny area if you take certain steps to ensure its success. The first step is to consider the weather of the entire season. Resist the urge to buy or seed dainty spring flowers in the cooler time of year if you know it is going to get much hotter later on. Always remember the dog days of summer are around the corner! This is hard to do, I know, when that multicolored ruffled spring pansy is calling your name . . .

There are many annuals or perennials to choose from that are sun and heat tolerant. For example, zinnias, native to Mexico, are reliable annual flowers for a sunny spot. They bloom in vivid colors in the summer. And established zinnias are almost drought tolerant! Likewise, the deer-resistant perennial red hot poker plant (*Kniphofia uvaria*) loves full sun and poor soils. They are suitable for USDA hardiness zones 5–9. And try the 10-inch-tall 'Arizona Sunset' hyssop (*Agastache aurantiaca* 'Arizona Sunset'), a perennial, with its minty fragrance. Goldfinches love the seed.

Another tip is to water your flower garden often and *deeply* during the heat of the summer. The key is to make sure the soil (not the flowers!) is fully moist. As I often say, it is the roots in the soil, not the flower petals, that need the water. Do not pass the hose rapidly over the flowers—you are simply watering the flower petals—it does nothing for your plants. And it's wasteful, because some of the water will simply evaporate. It is better to give the soil that the flowers are growing in a very thorough soaking. Connect a nozzle to your hose, turn it to the shower setting for a rain-like spray, and set it at the base of the plants. Let the water soak deeply into the earth. Do this two or three times a week. This is more effective than a quick spritz every day.

If your flowers are not particularly heat tolerant, they will appreciate a light misting of water in the air on a hot day. The mist cools down the sprayed area as it evaporates. So, for delicate flowers, set your hose nozzle on the mist setting and spray the air around them on a hot afternoon. Take care to do this well before evening, because the water may not evaporate later in the day and mildew can occur. By the way, misting will cool you down, too!

Mulching can help some woody perennials like Russian sage or lavender, but I do not mulch herbaceous flowers. Cover the soil with a *thin* layer of good organic mulch, such as finely ground bark or pine needles, around woody-stemmed flowers. This acts like a blanket between the soil and the hot sun and also helps to keep water in the ground.

Opposite page, bottom: Water in early morning or late afternoon because that is when plants do not have to deal with the heat and can really absorb the water. And it is the water-efficient thing to do—if you water during the hottest part of the day, up to 30 percent of the water simply evaporates from the heat.

26. CHERISH THE SOIL

The word *cultivate* derives from the Latin *colere*, which means both "to till" and "to cherish." I love that. When you turn over the soil and incorporate soil amendments, you are cultivating and cherishing it. How poetic.

Preparing the soil for growing plants is the most important step in making a beautiful garden of any kind. My advice to anyone who will listen is, "It is all about the soil." Make the soil a healthy, vibrant home for your flowers and they will thrive under your care. The idea is to feed the soil, not the plants. Take time to thoroughly amend the soil with organic nutrients before you bring out seeds for sowing or plants for planting. Do not skip this vital step! As the adage says, "You don't plant a ten dollar plant in a two dollar hole; you plant a two dollar plant in a ten dollar hole."

This saying may need to be adjusted for inflation, but it highlights the importance of the soil over the size of the plant. If the soil is full of life, then a small plant will grow happily in its new home. So, what to add to your garden bed to improve soil life and structure? Well, it depends on what you are planting and what you are starting with. Flowers that like rich, humusy soil that is moist but well drained may require well-rotted manure, leaf mold (composted leaves), earthworm castings, or compost. Other plants may like soil that is "lean," and these plants will need gravelly or gritty soil. This may mean adding sand, small stones, and perhaps some perlite. The major nutrients like nitrogen, phosphorus, and potassium are not helpful in lean soils.

Organic-based fertilizer or amendments enhance the soil's water-retention capabilities. I incorporate a healthy amount of compost in many flower beds. Other organic amendments to choose from include earthworm castings, fish and seaweed fertilizer, cottonseed meal, blood meal, manure, bone meal, and greensand. The amount and type of soil amendment you incorporate depends on your soil and plant. I use a diluted solution of nutrient-rich fish emulsion as a liquid fertilizer. It is a time-tested approach—the Pilgrims buried fish in the soil to ensure vigorous plant growth and plentiful harvests.

Talk to your local garden center or cooperative extension agent for advice. Spread the organic additives you choose on the surface of the soil and turn them over into the earth, deeply. Insert the shovel at least 12 inches into the soil. Do this at least twice, breaking up clods. Love the soil and it will love you right back.

Deep, dark soil in this garden makes the plants sing. Great soil is a boon to all gardening efforts.

Herbaceous plants have soft green stems. To a botanist, the word *herb* means any nonwoody plant. The banana tree is often mistaken as a tree or palm, but it is considered an herb. Interestingly, banana plants are herbaceous perennials that arise from an underground rhizome called a corm, and it takes 9 to 12 months from sowing to harvesting the fruit.

27. WHAT DOES *HERBACEOUS* MEAN?

In this book, I focus on herbaceous flowers. The word *herbaceous* describes plants that have a flexible, soft green stem. They are the opposite of woody plants, which include trees, shrubs, and vines that have stems that are not easily bendable and remain alive above ground even during the dormant season. They grow new shoots from the above-ground woody stems.

Herbaceous plants include those that have an annual, perennial, or biennial life cycle. Annual herbaceous plants are those that flower, set seed in one growing season, and do not regrow. Herbaceous perennial plants die to the ground at the end of the growing season, but parts of the plant survive underground and new growth develops the following year from these living tissues. They regenerate from the roots or from underground features such as bulbs, corms, rhizomes, and tubers.

Biennial plants differ from perennials in that they only have a two-year life cycle. They, too, stay alive underground in the winter and then in the next growing season they flower, go to seed, and die. Examples of flowering biennials include varieties of foxglove (*Digitalis*), hollyhock (*Alcea rosea*), and sweet William (*Dianthus barbatus*).

And then there are herbaceous evergreens. These plants are not woody but are evergreen plants with soft stems. Their leaves may remain visible during warm winters or in warmer growing zones. These include many hellebores, pulmonarias, some heucheras, epimediums, and geraniums. Hellebores, commonly known as Lenten rose, are herbaceous evergreen plants with thick, almost leathery leaves. They are prized for their early spring blooms and winter interest.

Hellebores have soft stems, but the tough, palmately arranged leaves can withstand cold weather. It's nodding flowers, known as Lenten roses, appear in late winter or early spring and are best viewed from a very close distance. The newer cultivars have upright flowers. Deer resistant.

28. SHOULD I CUT BACK IN WINTER OR NOT?

Most herbaceous perennials die back to ground level during the cold season, but some others may not disappear. Their stems and foliage remain standing, dried and brown, in late fall and early winter. Some gardeners may see this as unsightly debris and wonder if they should cut back the spent foliage. If you don't mind the look, and there is no disease present, you need not cut down these plants until late winter or early spring. In fact, it is now recommended to leave most perennials intact during winter instead of cutting them back to the ground. The stems and dried flowers add interest to the winter landscape, provide some insulation from the cold, and act as overwintering habitat for some birds, butterflies, and bee species.

Some perennials are sensitive to the cold, and these benefit from remaining intact overwinter. Do not cut back asters, Russian sage, red hot poker, lavender, chrysanthemums, and lady's mantle. Perennials with evergreen or semi-evergreen foliage should not be cut back until spring. These include foamflower, coral bells, and evergreen hellebores.

Other perennials should be left standing simply for their winter display interest, such as joe-pye weed. These stately plants add a new dimension to the dormant landscape. More important, the dried seed heads of certain flowers feed overwintering birds. So do not cut back purple or white coneflower with its oil-rich seeds, which goldfinches love. Also leave black-eyed Susan, sedum plants, globe thistle, and cup plant (*Silphium perfoliatum*) to dry naturally in the garden.

While some perennials like daylilies, irises, and peonies should be cut back to prevent disease and insect attack, many others should be allowed to remain standing over the winter. Just remember to cut them back in late winter to early spring before new growth emerges.

The late summer-blooming Russian sage (*Perovskia atriplicifolia*) has somewhat woody stems. You can leave the plant standing for winter interest. In the spring , prune it back to about 8 inches high before new growth starts

29. BECOME A "RAKE MASTER"

Raking the soil in a plant bed with a metal rake is a skill, an art to be mastered. I learned this, years ago, when I was a newbie in the world of professional horticulture. My boss was Alain Grumberg, a French gardener who had worked in the formal gardens of Versailles. He was a true professional and had little patience with my lack of raking ability. He would not let me touch a rake until I had watched him for weeks on end preparing the numerous flower beds in the expansive display garden at Mohonk Mountain House in New Paltz, New York. Like a chef handling a carving knife, he told me, you must learn how to use the tool properly.

In the early spring, we added a layer of aged horse manure and straw from a nearby barn to the existing beds. We turned over the soil using a rototiller. Then Alain raked the soil in each of the beds—first rough grading to take out larger stones and clods, then fine grading to smooth it out and remove smaller pebbles. Finally, he turned the rake over and used it, upside down, to press down on the edges around the perimeter of the plant bed. The rhythm of the strokes he made as he raked exhibited his command of the tool, holding it low to remove large stones, then raising it high to rake out smaller pebbles. It opened my eyes to the art of raking. I said to him, "You are a rake master."

I use that term now to impress upon others the importance of the rake in preparing plant beds. I suggest you aim to become a rake master. It takes a while. Practice makes perfect. And by the way, raking is a great form of exercise! Studies show that raking in the garden can burn between 200 and 224 calories per hour!

If you're only going to have one rake, choose a good-quality metal bow rake. It is shaped differently from a leaf rake. It has a curved bow that extends from both sides of the head, which gives the rake some spring action. The sturdiness of the head makes the bow rake the best tool for leveling and removing small stones from the soil. The metal tines are short and thick and can pull and mold the soil well. Get a professional-grade bow rake that will not come apart under pulling pressure.

If you have the wrong rake for your task, raking can be a chore. Do not use a leaf rake to grade the soil. It is designed to pick up lightweight leaves. A metal bow rake, as shown, is a workhorse tool and perfect for pulling heavy or damp soil. Another kind of grading rake is a lightweight aluminum rake. It has a wide head and a long handle. It is suitable for spreading loose soil and fine grading, but it will bend if used for heavier tasks.

30. A NOTE ABOUT PLANT NAMES

In these pages, I identify plants by their common name and botanical name. The latter is a two-part scientific name, genus and species. It is normally a Latin name, shown in italics and encased in parentheses following the common name, such as garden phlox (*Phlox paniculata*). Many common names may be easier to remember (and pronounce) than botanical names, but sometimes there are many common names for one plant, and this can become confusing. The botanical name, on the other hand, is used throughout the world to avoid difficulties of translation. Do not be intimated by the Latin names. You may already know many in your garden by their "first" botanical name (genus). For example, zinnias, allium, cosmos, chrysanthemums, and iris are a few that come to mind.

The genus is a unique category of plant. The species name that follows it is a descriptive word that may describe a plant's feature (such as color, bloom time, habitat, who discovered it, or place of origin). The other names that follow the genus and species names denote a naturally occurring variety that has one or more distinguishing characteristics and usually produces true-to-seed and/or a specially bred cultivar. The variety name always directly follows the species name. As for the cultivar, it will either follow the variety or the species name.

The word *cultivar* means a *culti*vated *var*iety—that is, a plant selected and cultivated by humans. Cultivar names are always surrounded by single quotation marks and are capitalized. An example of this is the Latin name for a coneflower cultivar: *Echinacea purpurea* 'Magnus.' Most flower cultivars are developed by plant breeders for unique flowers, leaf color, or growing habit. They normally do not reproduce true-to-seed. The term *spp.* at the end of some names indicates several species of a genus, such as *Begonia* spp.

This is a winter flowering begonia (*Begonia × hiemalis*). Botanical plant names include genus and species names, and they may also include variety and cultivar names. This plant is in the *Begonia* genus. The species name is *hiemalis*. The species name is descriptive of the plant. For example, the Latin term *hiemal* means "relating to winter." A genus name followed by an "×" means the plant is a cross between two different plant species—a hybrid plant.

31. WINTER HARDINESS—SO IMPORTANT TO KNOW

One of the most important things to know about a flowering plant is its climate hardiness. Cold temperatures can be fatal to tender flowers. Certain annual flowers and warm zone perennials can only be planted outside when nighttime temperature are reliably above 55 degrees. These tender plants do not overwinter in cooler climates. They grow for one season. If you want to plant permanent perennial flowers that come back every year, first determine if they are suited to your particular climate. You can do this by knowing the plant hardiness zone for your geographic area. This is shown on the United States Department of Agriculture (USDA) Plant Hardiness Zone Map. You can find this map online at planthardiness.ars.usda.gov/PHZMWeb.

The USDA Plant Hardiness Zone Map defines 13 zones by annual extreme minimum temperature (including Alaska, Hawaii, and Puerto Rico). Each growing zone is 10 degrees warmer (or colder) in an average winter than the adjacent zone. The higher the number, the warmer the zone. If you live in USDA hardiness zone 5 and a plant is rated for warmer USDA hardiness zones 7–10, then it is not hardy in your

Above: Lavender is native to dry hot areas of the Mediterranean. It loves heat and does not do well in humid weather or in cold, wet soils. If you live in an area where lavender is considered "marginally hardy" and want to increase its chances of survival, plant English lavender varieties in a protected, well-drained area such as in front of a southern-facing brick wall or near heat vents next to the house.

Left: In cold areas, snow helps to insulate many "marginally hardy" plants. Perennials that are considered marginally hardy can survive if they are covered with a solid blanket of snow for long periods in the winter. Unfortunately, icy conditions on the ground do not offer the same insulating benefits as snow does.

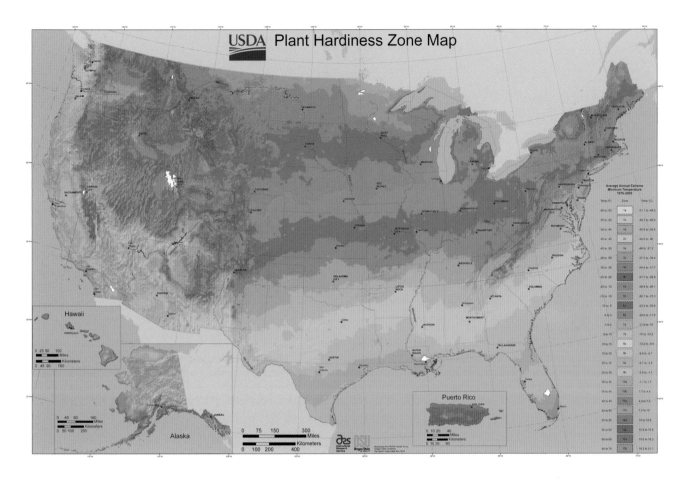

The US Department of Agriculture (USDA) Plant Hardiness Zone Map shows "hardiness zones" as strips of similar climate that run roughly east to west across the country (except in the high mountains and coasts). Zone 3 has an average annual lowest temperature of -40 to -30°F, while zone 10 has lows of only 30 to 40°F. *Map by US Department of Agriculture.*

area. These zones are broken into *a* (hardier) and *b* (less hardy) subzones.

The hardiness map is based on the *average* minimum winter temperatures. This may not be accurate in certain very cold years. For example, some plants can withstand 20-degree temperatures for a few hours overnight, but if this temperature lasts for several days, or if it occurs more than once during the season, then the plants may succumb to the cold. For this reason, keep an eye on your local area's minimal temperatures in the winter—lower valley areas may stay

cold while higher elevations do not. And areas by bodies of water can be a few degrees warmer than inland areas. These minor differences can affect a plant's viability.

The amount of precipitation can also affect a plant's hardiness. Some plants can survive cold temperatures but cannot tolerate winter moisture. For example, hardy English lavender (*Lavandula angustifolia*) varieties such as 'Hidcote' or 'Munstead' can grow in USDA hardiness zone 5, but cold wet roots can negate this rating.

32. TRY A FLOWER HIGHWAY TO CONTROL INSECT PESTS

We all know that pesticides are poison and that we must limit their use in our gardens and farms. But how to control plant pests? One option is to plant flowers! According to the business magazine *Fast Company*, some organic farmers are growing flowers that attract good bugs that, in turn, eat bad bugs. This is why farmers plant wide strips of flowers within the rows of their crops and around the perimeter of farmland. The flowers they plant are particularly favored by insects that devour destructive pests. These long "flower highways" travel close to the crops so the good bugs can easily find the bad insects to eat.

They reported, "In one study in Switzerland, researchers planted poppies, cilantro, dill, and other flowers along fields of winter wheat. The plants fed and sheltered insects like ladybugs that ate the bugs that eat wheat, and ultimately reduced leaf damage by 61 percent." Growing the right mix of flowers can increase yield and is economically smart.

Wildflower habitats are also being planted around edges of golf courses to attract good insects such as native bees. In general, native bees will only sting if antagonized, so they do not pose a threat to golfers. The most effective edge plantings, they found, are ones with the highest "floral richness." These wildflower strips increased biological control rates in adjacent turfgrass areas by up to 50 percent, according to the study "Floral abundance and richness drive beneficial arthropod conservation and biological control on golf course" in the journal *Urban Ecosystems*. In other words, flowers are the best attractors for good bugs. Try this for yourself with a mix of perennial, native wildflowers that bloom from April to October: coneflowers, columbines, black-eyed Susans, clover, hyssop, and goldenrod.

Planting flowers as a pest-control measure is an important step in our evolving natural gardening practices. For example, ladybugs eat destructive pests like aphids, mites, and scale. So plant flowers that ladybugs like, such as angelica, calendula, chamomile, chives, cilantro, cosmos, dill, fennel, feverfew, goldenrod, signet marigold, and yarrow. If you plant it, they will come. Include a flower highway in your garden.

Top, left: Feverfew (*Tanacetum parthenium*), a medicinal herb, has small white daisy-like blooms above light green foliage. Feverfew's pungent foliage emits a strong, bitter odor that repels bees. It attracts other good bugs such as hoverflies and tachinid flies. These insects eat pests like aphids, thrips, and mealybugs that ravage garden plants. Do not plant feverfew near flowers that rely on bees for pollination!

Top, right: Ladybugs eat destructive insect pests, so invite ladybugs into your garden with the annual flower they love, cosmos (*Cosmos bipinnatus*). The flowers come in white, red, and pink, all with a yellow center. They are easy to grow and their open petals make great landing pads for ladybugs.

Bottom: Sweet alyssum (*Lobularia maritima*), with its lovely fragrance, attracts the aphid-eating hoverfly. Hoverflies have yellow and black stripes and hover over flowers. They love to feed on the pollen and nectar of sweet alyssum and then lay their eggs on the undersides of the leaves near aphid colonies. The voracious hoverfly larvae then eat the aphids. Interplant sweet alyssum everywhere in your garden. Hoverflies also like coriander, candytuft, and pincushion flower.

33. THE PLANT BED, CROWNED

Flower beds should never be flat. They should be sculpted and made slightly higher in the center. Each flower bed that I create, if it is not on a slope, is "crowned" with a gentle slope down to all sides. This is very similar to the profile of a street where the center of the road is higher so that rainwater drains down to both sides of the road.

The basic principle here is to let water penetrate in the soil but to drain the excess water slowly away. If the surface is flat, then the water will remain and puddle in the low places. The result is that the flowers planted in these low areas may suffer from too much water accumulating around their roots. The key is to let water drain off. Crowning the bed is the best way to accomplish this.

You will need a sufficient amount of soil to make a plant bed higher in the center by a few inches. Do not skimp on this part. If you do not have an adequate quantity of good topsoil on hand, you must get it from another place on your site or bring it in. This is when the task of crowning a plant bed becomes a real chore. Using quality soil is a must. Know where your topsoil is coming from! I cannot stress this enough. Do not bring in "fill" dirt or phony "topsoil" created from silty "pond bottom" soil. I know it is tempting not to crown a bed, but all I can say is that you will get the best results if you do. It is all about the soil—its quality and how you grade it.

When creating a flower bed, make sure the center is higher than the edges. Use a spade for edging. It has a sharpened, flat edge designed for cutting through soil and roots. It is the perfect tool when a clean line and precise angle are needed. Edge the bed after you have contoured it to a crown, as shown here.

34. SWEET SOIL OR SOUR SOIL—WHY IT IS SO IMPORTANT

I remember the first time I heard someone say their garden had sweet soil. I was young, and I was afraid to ask if that meant it was somewhat sugary. I later learned that sweet soil means the soil is alkaline. By contrast, acidic soil is considered to be sour. This understanding is very important, because when a plant has health problems it is often the result of the soil's degree of acidity or alkalinity. Come to think of it—that is true for us as well.

In fact, the level of a soil's acidity, or its pH, should be the first thing a gardener checks. This is because if the soil is too acidic or too alkaline, many nutrients cannot be released to the plants. So no matter how much you fertilize, the food may not be available to the plant roots.

The term *pH* basically means the "power of hydrogen." The pH scale, the standard measurement of acidity, was developed in 1909. It measures the amount of hydrogen ions in a solution. Soil with a pH measurement lower than 7.0 is an acidic soil, and soil with a pH higher than 7.0 is an alkaline soil. Most landscape and garden plants do best at pH values between 6.5 and 7.2. It is when the levels go above or below these numbers that problems occur. For example, extremely acidic soils can cause blighted leaf tips, yellowing of foliage, and stunted growth. Extremely alkaline soils can cause iron chlorosis, a yellowing of the leaves but with green veins. It is caused by iron deficiency. Alkaline soils can also cause bud drop in gardenias.

Flowers that prefer slightly acidic soil include petunias, calibrachoa, gerbera, pansy, and snapdragon. Flowers that like slightly alkaline soil are zinnias, clematis, hosta, echinacea, salvia, phlox, dianthus, baby's breath, and lavender.

The pH of a soil can be inexpensively tested by a soil laboratory. County extension service agents can give advice on where to have soil samples analyzed. You can also purchase soil pH test kits at your local garden center.

Organic soils are very successful in balancing acidic and alkaline properties. Some forms of organic matter that you may add to the soil can be acidifying, but this acidity is minor when compared to the application of acid-forming fertilizers and high-intensity rainfalls.

"Remember that children, marriages, and flower gardens reflect the kind of care they get."
—H. Jackson Brown Jr.

35. DROUGHT TOLERANT—WHAT THAT MEANS

In dry seasons or dry areas, watering flowers can be a chore. More important, it can be a waste of water, which is a precious resource. The solution to this dilemma is to plant drought-tolerant flowers. Notice I didn't say drought-proof or drought resistant, because all plants need some water. But there are certain flowers that can survive a short-term lack of moisture better than others. In fact, some drought-tolerant flowers prefer to be on the dry side and do not appreciate too much water. If water is scarce, select annual and perennial flowers that don't mind drought stress.

When you plant with drought tolerance in mind, you are saving water and practicing water-wise gardening. This means you should choose flowers that do not need additional water and can survive in the heat of summer—using plants that have lower supplemental water needs. To save on maintenance time you can group plants by their water needs. Water-wise gardeners are leading the way into the 21st century. Look for drought-tolerant flowers when you select which ones to grow in your garden.

Many drought-tolerant flowers need sun, but some flowers can handle both shade and dry conditions. Dry shade is one of the most difficult planting sites, and it is hard to find flowers suitable for this condition. Some perennial flowers that are dry shade tolerant include hellebore, foamflower, and perennial geranium, such as *Geranium macrorrhizum* 'Bevan's Variety.' The last example flourishes for years. It is also one of the best ground covers that I have found for dry shady areas.

Portulaca, also known as moss rose, is a great drought-tolerant annual flower. It thrives in dry, poor soil and warm temperatures due to its thick succulent leaves. The cup-shaped flowers come in a variety of vibrant colors. Drought-tolerant perennials include anise hyssop (*Agastache*), yarrow (*Achillea*), golden marguerite (*Anthemis tinctoria*), and false indigo (*Baptisia*).

Top: 'Biokovo' perennial geranium (*Geranium cantabrigiense* 'Biokovo') grows to about 1 foot tall and spreads out. It is a dense, deer-resistant ground cover that has starry white blooms accented by pink sepals in late spring through summer. 'Biokovo' bears glossy green fragrant foliage that turns an attractive reddish hue in fall. It thrives in full- to part-shade conditions. Hardy in Zones 5–8. 2015 Perennial Plant Association Plant of the Year!

Bottom, left: *Portulaca grandiflora* is commonly called moss rose, which well describes its ruffled and vividly colored 1-inch flowers. This annual is a succulent that typically grows to 6 to 8 inches tall and spreads to 12 inches wide. The flowers appear on prostrate stems and form a mosslike foliage mat. It does well in poor, dry soils and in drought. The moss rose flowers bloom in hot full sun, from summer to frost. They close at night and on cloudy days.

Bottom, right: Lantana (*Lantana camara*) is drought tolerant. It is a warm-climate perennial plant grown as an annual in cooler areas. Its flowers burst with rainbow colors in wonderful combinations. It blooms continuously through the summer until early fall. Lantana loves sun and heat. It is an excellent flower to attract butterflies, deer resistant. Zones 8–10.

36. SELF-SEEDERS! FREE FLOWERS! BE CAREFUL.

Self-seeding is a way Nature ensures that flowers keep returning. Self-seeders are plants that freely disperse their seeds to germinate and eventually pop up all over the place. Seed them once, and they return, via new seeds, each year. These self-sown plants sometimes grow in unwanted places, but it is relatively easy to transplant or remove them. Beginning gardeners can't fail with vigorous self-seeders—they don't require much, and they bring an element of surprise to your landscape.

Some gardeners frown on self-seeding flowers because their random appearances upset the orderliness of a flower border. Others embrace self-seeding because it is a gardening technique that works with Nature to develop a "cultivated wildness" and a less fussy garden. Self-sowers may be annuals, biennials, or short-lived perennials. You can sow the seeds directly onto the soil. After that, watch as Nature does her thing. Left alone, prolific seeders let you "intermingle" plants that flower and mature at different times, which creates interest throughout the year. To do this, let the seed heads of self-seeders ripen fully. Do not deadhead the flowers! The seed capsules dry out on the plant and eventually split open to release tiny seeds. You can harvest the ripened, brown capsules and scatter seeds wherever you want new flowers to grow. Some seedlings may be slow to emerge, and some may need a period of cold before they germinate. Patience is necessary.

Some annual flowers are prolific self-seeders. These can become invasive if you are not careful. But if you manage these seedlings, you will always have something in bloom with little effort. Annual self-seeders include the old-fashioned spider flower (*Cleome*), German chamomile (*Matricaria recutita*), bachelor's buttons (*Centaurea cyanus*), tall verbena (*Verbena bonariensis*), sweet alyssum (*Lobularia maritima*), and love-in-a-mist (*Nigella damascena*). The same holds true for biennials and perennials such as foxgloves (*Digitalis* var.), bleeding heart (*Lamprocapnos spectabilis*), Lenten rose (*Helleborus orientalis*), white wood aster (*Eurybia divaricata*), columbine (*Aquilegia*), and forget-me-not (*Myosotis sylvatica*). Try the hardy perennial 'Jackpot' snow daisy (*Tanacetum niveum* 'Jackpot'), for masses of white self-sowing flowers. Before sowing, make sure your choices are not listed as a noxious weed in your area.

Left: The small, daisy-like flowers of forget-me-nots (*Myosotis sylvatica*) are rampant self-seeders. They are listed as a noxious weed in some Midwestern states so be careful with them. They thrive in moist areas with morning sun. They come in shades of blue, yellow, or white, often with yellow or white eyes. Forget-me-nots look best planted in groups in rock gardens, beds, or in borders. Zones 3–8.

Below: 'Sweet William' catchfly (*Silene armeria*) is a tough, hardy perennial that easily self-sows. It will pop up in the garden everywhere. It is native to Europe but has naturalized in parts of the United States. Its vivid rose-pink rounded flower clusters appear in summer on 12- to 16-inch-tall upright stems. It likes full sun with excellent drainage. It does not do well in high humidity and heat. Zones 5–8.

Opposite: Eastern red columbine (*Aquilegia canadensis*) is a short-lived native perennial with showy red-and-yellow nodding flowers with long narrow spurs. It blooms in late spring/ early summer in sun to part shade. It likes well-drained but moist soil and grows 1 to 2 feet tall. Red columbine self-sows its abundant seeds, and new plants then pop up between rocks or in woodlands. Scatter columbine seeds in bare areas—it is deer and rabbit resistant. The cultivar 'Little Lanterns' is half the height of the regular species. Very attractive to hummingbirds. Zones 4–8.

37. MINDFUL WEEDING

Hand weeding, as Christopher Lloyd, a 20th-century British gardener and author, reminded us, can be a kind of meditation. It requires focus, but not much thought, so it lets our minds roam as we perform this needed chore. Some people might say "let the weeds have their way," but in a flower garden this is not wise. Weeds such as plantains, chickweed, and stiltgrass, compete for moisture and nutrients in the soil and may, therefore, inhibit flowers' growth. Also, once established, weeds are hard to remove. It is smart to pull them out, roots and all, before they overrun the garden.

The best time to hand weed is after a good rain. The moist soil allows the roots to come out easily with a steady tug at the base of the plant. If you pull out weeds in dry soil, the stem will often snap off just below the surface, leaving the roots in place. This allows the weed to continue growing. If you cannot wait for a rainstorm, then water the soil deeply before you weed. This will make your job so much easier, and you will be free to think big thoughts—or plan your next trip—while you work.

Weeding is often a solitary activity. If you prefer company, then I say have a "weeding party." Invite some gardening pals over and promise them a lovely lunch if they give you half an hour of weeding time. Companionship makes the work go so much faster.

So turn off the cell phone. Take some deep breaths. Look closely at your garden and, as you pull out the pesky weeds, enjoy the moment.

"Many gardeners will agree that hand-weeding is not the terrible drudgery that it is often made out to be. Some people find in it a kind of soothing monotony. It leaves their minds free to develop the plot for their next novel or to perfect the brilliant repartee with which they should have encountered a relative's latest example of unreasonableness."

—CHRISTOPHER LLOYD,
THE WELL-TEMPERED GARDEN

38. ORGANIC WEED CONTROL

Flower gardens can be relatively minimum maintenance if you control the weeds from the very start—weeds rob nutrients and water from your flowering plants. So how to fully remove those pesky weeds? Chemical weed control harms the environment in many ways. Using the sun to bake the weeds, a process called solarization, kills the weed seeds but also kills the good organisms in the soil that you want. Some suggest using common household items such as salt, vinegar, or Epsom salts to kill weeds, but these too can be harmful to the beneficial organisms in the soil. The aim is to remove the weeds while maintaining and promoting healthy soil.

So, what to do? First, choose plants that are fungus resistant and plant them close together to crowd out insidious weeds. You can also use plants to cover bare spots where weeds can take hold. And you should practice simple, time-proven weed cultivation using weeding tools, such as a heavy-duty weeding hoe. Nutsedges and purslane, both perennial weeds, tend to be especially resilient. The best method for eliminating them is by hand pulling.

A timely weed-prevention practice is to cut off weed flowers before they set seed. You may leave the weed but at least remove the flowers and future seeds. And definitely use a weed-free mulch and apply it early in the spring before annual weeds germinate. Pile fallen leaves in a layer 2 to 3 inches thick in the fall and this will be great mulch the following spring. Timing is so important! Don't apply mulch too late in the spring, otherwise the weeds will germinate and grow through the mulch. Don't use treated lawn clippings if the turf was treated with herbicides or chemical fertilizer products. And finally, don't over-mulch because you risk suffocating the plants. This last reminder applies to flowers, shrubs, and trees.

When removing weeds with long taproots such as dandelions, it is important to get the whole root. If you miss a small piece of root, the weed will regrow. A tool such as a dandelion weeder can help.

39. THE MEADOW GARDEN—THE SECRET IS POOR SOIL

Meadow gardens are magical: open sunny areas that blend meadow grasses with flowering plants. These "wild" gardens provide food and habitat for birds, butterflies, and insects. And they delight us with a loose display of colorful blossoms. Meadow gardens were once considered to be weedy, but thanks to people like the great 20th-century English plantsman and author, Christopher Lloyd, we now appreciate them in all their unwieldy glory. Lloyd's willingness to let plants sow themselves and settle wherever they like opened people's eyes to a new way of flower gardening. He wrote about his meadow garden in his famous garden at Great Dixter in England, "Your first sight, on entering the front gate, is of two areas of rough grass, either side of the path to the house. . . . They contain a rich assortment of plants that enjoy growing in turf and the grass is not cut until all its contents have completed ripening and shedding their seed. Much of this is native material that needed no introduction. The poorer the soil, the richer the tapestry that can be created."

The key, as Lloyd noted, is the poor soil! Wildflowers can grow in less-than-ideal soil conditions while weeds do not. So do not enrich the soil in your meadow garden, and help the wildflowers win out over the weeds. This is also true for grasses. They will not overwhelm wildflowers in lean soil.

Left: Rocket larkspur (*Consolida ajacis*) is true to its name, as spikes of upright pink, blue, purple, or white flowers arise from a base of low-growing leaves. It is a stunning wildflower and a perfect annual for a meadow garden. This plant spreads by reseeding itself. Deer resistant. Plant and seeds are poisonous. Blooms from spring to summer and grows in disturbed areas and a wide range of well-drained soil conditions. Hardy in zones 2–11.

Opposite page: Red corn poppies (*Papaver rhoeas*) and blue cornflowers (*Centaurea cyanus*) are a natural combination in a meadow garden. They are annuals but self-seed and come back anew each year in disturbed soil. The colorful poppies, with their tissue-paper petals, seem to dance on the breeze. The cornflowers in the distance, also known as bachelor's buttons, appear like blue confetti. These two plants are extremely easy to grow from seed strewn about in the fall. Cut them down each year in late October, after the flowers have seeded the area.

Why not plant some sunflowers outside a west-facing window? Sunflowers are heliotropic, meaning that they follow the sun. They always face east when the flower heads are filled with seed. They will happily greet you as you gaze outside on summer days.

40. FLOWERS THAT FOLLOW THE SUN

Heliotropic flowers, such as sunflowers and calendulas, are known for their ability to track the sun as it moves from east to west during the day. Young sunflower (*Helianthus annuus*) buds and leaves follow the sun then swing back to the east overnight. When the sunflower blossoms, the stem stiffens and it no longer moves. The seed head remains facing east toward the sun as the seeds develop. The common field marigold (*Calendula arvensis*) of central and southern Europe does the same—it traverses a 19-degree arc from east to west every day, seemingly following the movement of the sun.

Heliotropism of flowers and leaves illustrates how plants have adapted to their environment in ingenious ways. In cold climates, heliotropic flowers that face east in the morning heat up more quickly than west-facing flowers. This added warmth attracts bees and other pollinators which, studies have found, prefer warmer flowers in the morning. This finding confirms the old gardeners' advice to grow vegetable and flower gardens with a full exposure to eastern sunlight and the morning sun. Plants seem to grow better when they receive early morning light. They warm up faster, the dew dries off quicker, and pollinators visit the warm flowers facing the rising sun before any others.

You can see heliotropism at work with the fragrant annual heliotrope (*Heliotropium arborescens*), Iceland poppies (*Papaver nudicaule*), and an alpine plant known as the snow buttercup (*Ranunculus adoneus*). The yellow-orange blossoms of the California poppy (*Eschscholzia californica*) also follow the sun. Heliotropism shows us that plants are more active than we think. So grow heliotropic flowers and enjoy the movement.

The bright, yellow-orange blossoms of the California poppy (*Eschscholzia californica*) follow the sun. They open as the sun's rays touch the blossoms and close as dusk descends. This annual has flowers atop finely cut silvery green foliage. Blooms over a long period. Drought tolerant. These poppies reseed themselves every year. Hardy in zones 5–10; it's a perennial in the warmer climates of zones 8–10.

41. KEEPING FLOWERS UPRIGHT

Staking flowers is viewed as a nuisance, but sometimes you need to keep tall growing annuals and perennials from falling over as they grow. You can handle leaning stems by providing stronger plants for the flowers to rest upon. Good choices include grasses, shrubs, and bushy perennials. Such a scheme requires planning ahead of time and is not always possible. So learning ways to stake and support tall flowers is the way to go.

Some flowering annuals and perennials are not as sturdy as others. If these flowers are overfertilized, their stems grow lush and weak. These flowers will need support. When you stake a growing flower after it starts to flop, you are undertaking what is known as remedial staking. Simply insert a support such as a bamboo stake, single stake, or sturdy branch into the ground beside the flowers. The top of the stake should be somewhere between the midpoint of plant's current height and its peak growing point. Use soft jute or green hemp twine to gather the flowers and tie them loosely to the stake. Natural twine is better than green covered wire ties because twine eventually disintegrates.

The other kind of staking is called preventive staking. Insert stakes in early spring before plants need them. Drive the stakes deep into the soil to anchor them. You can use cut twigs from fast-growing plants such as willows or red twig dogwood, or you can use bamboo stakes. You can fashion a grid or a corral around emerging stems, using twine to hold the stakes together. Another type of support consists of creating a network of well-branched twigs or brush around the young plants. Insert them deeply in the ground and the plants will grow through this tangle and use it

for support. The growth will eventually hide it from view.

Of course, you can use a fence as a support or insert metal plant rings or metal supports.

Bushy clematis is similar to the familiar, vining clematis that climbs up lamp posts. But bushy clematis does not climb. It has a rambling habit and will sprawl if no support is added. The flowers of the deer-resistant bushy clematis appear on new strong shoots each spring. The stems die back to the ground after frost. Stake or contain the young stems. Here is a rustic structure, made from small branches and tied with jute twine that surrounds bushy clematis in Stonecrop Gardens in Cold Spring, New York. The variety, *Clematis recta* Purpurea, has purple foliage and masses of small, starry white flowers. Grows 3 to 4 feet high. Hardy in zones 4–8.

Luffa vines (*Luffa aegyptiaca*) growing on the fence at the Vegetable Garden in Harry P. Leu Gardens in Orlando, Florida. Luffa is a type of annual tropical or subtropical gourd that can be dried and used as a body scrubber. The climbing vines bear ornamental yellow flowers. They grow fast and work well when trained along a fence, as shown. Luffa can be grown from small plants in zone 6 gardens or from seed in zone 7 and higher. Most plants in the squash family are natural climbers.

42. WHY GROW NATIVE FLOWERS?

Did you know that flowers that are native to your area require less water than most non-natives once they are established? They are also better at resisting native pests and diseases than non-native flowers, and they need less fertilizer. Last, but most important, they are part of the natural ecosystem of birds, bees, moths, and more, and they are a natural food source for them. It is a smart move to grow more native flowers—they require less care, place less stress on our resources, and are desired by your local pollinators.

What defines a native plant? Answers are elusive, because people have been moving plants around for thousands of years. That said, native plants are those that occur naturally in a region in which they evolved. They are the ecological basis of life in their area. Without these plants, and the insects that coevolved with them, local birds cannot survive.

More natives in the flower garden is the way to go. They are low maintenance, offer beautiful flowers, produce colorful fruits and seeds, and naturally express the life cycle of a garden as the seasons progress. They conserve water, provide erosion control, and are a source of nectar for pollinators, including hummingbirds, native bees, and butterflies.

The key to success when growing native flowers is to match the right plants to your site. For example, a backyard with at least six hours of full sun in USDA hardiness zones 5–7 can be filled with purple coneflower, blazing star, New England aster, baptisia, black-eyed Susan, bee balm, and goldenrod. The soil conditions are important, too. Therefore, do not plant swamp milkweed or blue lobelia on a dry site; likewise, plants suited to dry shade should not be planted in a wetland area.

A comprehensive resource for learning more about native plants is the PLANTS Database website (plants.sc.egov.usda.gov/java), published by the Natural Resources Conservation Service (NRCS).

Top, left: A flower native to swampy, moist areas is the cardinal flower (*Lobelia cardinalis*). It is named for the pure red color of its flowers, which is similar to the color of the vestments worn by Roman Catholic cardinals. Spires of late-summer flowers open from the bottom to top. Good for rain gardens, along streams, and edges of ponds in full sun or part shade. Hardy in zones 3–9.

Top, right: Our native great blue cardinal flower (*Lobelia siphilitica*) is the blue counterpart of the red cardinal flower (*Lobelia cardinalis*). It is a desirable plant for woodland gardens with its blue blooms in late summer. It likes moist conditions and damp clay soil. It is shown here with the native perennial hairy alumroot (*Heuchera villosa*), with its feathery, plume-like flower spikes. Zones 4–8.

Bottom, left: Dense blazing star (*Liatris spicata* var. *resinosa*) is a native perennial that does best in moist conditions. Its tall lavender spikes are on full display in sunny areas in midsummer to fall. In full bloom, *Liatris spicata* produces nectar and pollen for bees, hummingbirds, butterflies, and moths. Researchers suspect blazing star produces chemical cues that draw monarch butterflies to their floral spires. Blazing star grows 24 to 48 inches tall and can fit in any native garden. It combines well with the flowers of Stokes' aster (*Stokesia laevis*). Deer resistant! Zones 3–9.

Bottom, right: Butterfly weed (*Asclepias tuberosa*) is the food source for monarch and gray hairstreak butterfly caterpillars. This native perennial is both beautiful and useful! It was named the 2017 Perennial Plant of the Year by the Perennial Plant Association. Its flat-topped clusters of bright orange flowers, and the droves of pollinators it draws, have made this a popular flower in perennial gardens. It is drought tolerant and likes the sun and well-drained sandy soils. Requires little care once established. Zones 3–9.

"To plant is but a part of landscape composition;
to co-ordinate is all."
—CHRISTOPHER TUNNARD

FLOWER GARDEN DESIGN TIPS & GREEN THOUGHTS

It is easy to plant a flower garden, right? The colorful flowers all blend to make a beautiful scene. On one level, that is correct—flowers can make a garden "sing." But to coordinate the overall composition for a striking flower garden requires some planning. For example, you may choose to add fine-leaved grasses for contrast or insert a tall obelisk for some height. Other possibilities include limiting the color scheme to two main colors or planting only native flowering plants. In this chapter, I suggest flower combinations and design tips to enhance your flower gardening efforts. It really is about planning before you plant, as the 20th-century Canadian-born landscape architect Christopher Tunnard opined.

If there is one piece of advice I can share about composing a flower garden, it is to plan it as you would a painting—spreading out color and texture, balancing it all visually. Consider the heights, the time of flowering, and the cultural needs. And do not be afraid to experiment! You can always move flowering herbaceous plants around if you don't mind the extra effort.

Another pointer: make sure the site and soil are suitable for the flowers you use. They will thrive if you offer them an appropriate home.

Do not plant shade-loving plants in a hot western exposure and vice versa. Do not overfertilize flowers that like lean soil. Flowers are living things and their growing needs come before all.

I have also included some musings about flowers and gardening in this chapter. My "green thoughts" are gleaned from a life spent out in the field as a landscape designer and gardener. These thoughts highlight the effect of Nature on our well-being, but most of all they celebrate the joy of gardening.

Above: Black-eyed Susans are summer's calling card.

Left: Brick-red bearded iris and shrub roses form the foreground, with a colorful flower border of 'Walker's Low' catmint, and yellow 'Goldmound' Japanese spirea in the distance. The white flowering trees are kousa dogwoods. By Johnsen Landscapes & Pools.

Opposite page: The upright showy flower spikes of white perennial wood sage (*Salvia x sylvestris* 'Snow Hill') bloom from late spring to early summer. It is effective in drifts and mixed flower beds. Zones 4–8. It looks great planted with the globes of spring-blooming purple allium. Both are deer resistant.

43. FLOWERS ARE LIVING THINGS

> "Flowers are the music of the ground
> from earth's lips spoken without sound."
> —EDWIN CURRAN

Flowers have a life of their own—they grow and bloom according to an inborn schedule and, in so doing, brighten our days. We, gardeners, enjoy their "aliveness" and grow both annual and perennial flowers in plant beds, along fences, bordering our walks, or in a vase. We tip them back, pull out errant seedlings, and apply water when needed. Flower gardening helps us connect with the green world in a beautiful way.

Sometimes the understanding that "flowers are plants" is lost to more lofty notions of art, design, and composition. Beware of this trap. Some people may become so involved with flowers as an artistic medium that they forget they are living plants. Roberto Burle Marx, the great 20th-century Brazilian landscape designer, reminded us of this in his 1962 lecture, "The Garden as a Form of Art." Said Marx: "One may think of a plant as a brushstroke, as a single stitch of embroidery; but one must never forget that it is a living thing."

Burle Marx was instrumental in defining 20th-century modern landscape design. He was a great artist-designer and an innovative plantsman. He exemplified, in his long career, the blending of artistic and ecological concerns. Today the awareness that plants are living things is imperative. No longer can we impose our will upon the earth without being mindful of the consequences of our actions. Chemical fertilizers adversely affect microscopic life in the soil. Insecticides kill more than pesky pests. We are not alone in our gardening endeavors; we are literally co-creating with Nature.

So as you plant flowers in your garden, in whichever way you choose, remember that artistic expression and growing healthy flowers are not mutually exclusive. They are one together. That is the essence of great flower garden design.

The Japanese windflower 'Honorine Jobert' (Anemone hybrid 'Honorine Jobert') was named the PPA's 2016 Perennial Plant of the Year. It does best when planted in partial shade, or protected from hot afternoon sun. These tough perennials will naturalize and form a colony over time. Zones 4–8.

44. FLOWERS MIX WELL WITH GRASSES

Ornamental grasses are becoming a staple in our landscapes, and for good reason—they are easy to grow, and their slender blades, with their height, grace, and movement, add an artful contrast to other plants. Best of all, grasses are deer resistant. These unique qualities make ornamental grasses a true asset in a flower garden.

Herbaceous flowers mix especially well with grasses. To choose the right grass as a companion to a flower, determine the full height of the specific grass before you plant it. That small wispy grass plant may grow to be 6 feet tall! Also check with your local cooperative extension agency to be sure that the plant is not invasive in your area.

Lastly, make sure the grass is not a cool season grass that flourishes in spring but that can melt and go dormant in summer, just when heat-loving flowers planted next to it are at their best.

You have many ornamental grasses to consider growing with summer flowers. Consider planting Japanese forest grass (*Hakonechloa macra* 'Aureola'), which is a compact, USDA hardiness zone 6 plant with drooping yellow leaf blades; and 'Karl Foerster' feather reed grass (*Calamagrostis × acutiflora* 'Karl Foerster'), which is a tall, strongly vertical grass with feathery stalks that ripen to a wheat color in fall. It is rated for USDA hardiness zones 5–9. Another winner, among many,

The narrow, vertical plumes of the 4- to 6-feet-tall feather reed grass (*Calamagrostis × acutiflora* Stricta) mix beautifully with the multicolored, airy, daisy-like blooms of 'Sensation Mix' cosmos (*Cosmos bipinnatus* 'Sensation Mix'), an annual flower. The upright reed grass is only 18 inches wide, flowering in mid-June. 'Karl Foerster' is a popular variety of feather reed grass. Foliage reaches 1½ to 2 feet tall and wide; bloom stalks reach 6 feet tall. Hardy in zones 5–9.

Left: The annual Zinnia 'Profusion Yellow' blooms nonstop all summer with 2-inch flowers on a vigorous 12- to 15-inch-tall plant. The bold yellow petals surround an eye-catching central cone. Here, it peeks out in front of dwarf fountain grass (*Pennisetum alopecuroides* 'Hameln'). This is a great combination for a sunny summer and fall garden.

Right: Red-tipped 'Haense Herms' switchgrass (*Panicum virgatum* 'Haense Herms') makes a soft contrast in front of pink coneflowers. Its green foliage has a strong red color by September and stays red until frost. It grows to 3 feet tall. Perennial ornamental grasses offer varied colors and textures, which make them a popular addition to a flower garden. Zones 2–9.

is 'Northwind' switchgrass (*Panicum virgatum* 'Northwind'). It has wide, olive-green foliage that in September is topped with attractive narrow plumes. 'Northwind' grows 4 to 6 feet tall in USDA hardiness zones 5–9.

A vase-shaped grass that I often plant with flowers is 'Morning Light' maiden grass (*Miscanthus sinensis* 'Morning Light'). It makes a lovely, free-flowing companion, and its delicate silver variegated foliage catches the light in the garden. It has silky light plumes that have a pink blush. Leave this grass standing during the winter for interest. It is suitable for USDA hardiness zones 5–9.

45. ROCKS. FLOWERS. ACTION.

Flower gardens can be quiet places for relaxation and renewal. To help create a more zen-like atmosphere, a few well-placed rocks among the flowers will do the trick. Why rocks? Because they are Nature's most enduring material and add a still presence to the landscape. They are a solid counterbalance to short-lived flower displays. And more important, rocks serve as warming spots for butterflies, our flower pollinators, to bask on in the summer sun.

There are many ways to combine rocks with flowers. Traditional rock gardens are one example, but there are other design options. You can simply place one or more large rocks within a flower bed, or at its edges, or both. Flowers that drape over the stones are a definite eye catcher. Or plant a large group of tall-growing flowers behind a large rock or low-growing ones at its base. You can also set several long, narrow stones vertically within a flower bed to act as dramatic "standing stones." All of these approaches highlight the contrast of hard rock and soft flowers. Rocks ground us and flowers elevate us. It is this dynamic juxtaposition that makes this arrangement so compelling.

I prefer to collect and use rocks from a garden's

The low-growing, soft blue blossoms of floss flower (*Ageratum houstonianum*) contrast well with the light-colored rock behind them. Ageratum adds a fuzzy blue accent next to 'Titan Apricot' annual vinca (*Catharanthus roseus* 'Titan Apricot'), as shown here. I often plant these annual flowers together because both are deer resistant and bloom from late spring to first frost in a sunny location.

Above left: Pink New Guinea impatiens, a strong performing annual, crowd together next to a craggy rock. The soft blossoms blend well with the hard stone. The thin-bladed grass on the right is 'Evergold' sedge.

Above, right: Rocky sites do not deter the common orange daylily (*Hemerocallis fulva*). This summer-flowering perennial is native to Asia, and it is tolerant of any soil. It is easy to grow and naturalizes, so you may see it blooming along roadsides. Grows up to 4 feet tall. Zones 2–9.

Left: The bright golden-yellow flowers of the perennial 'Zagreb' threadleaf tickseed (*Coreopsis verticillata* 'Zagreb') are borne on slender green stems, growing to 12 inches high. The dainty flowers continuously bloom from early summer through fall. The finely cut foliage of this hardy plant makes an interesting contrast with rocks in a sunny garden. Zones 3–9.

site rather than bring them in from somewhere else. These native rocks resonate with the land. I know it is not always possible to do this, but it is a good practice if you have a lot of stone at hand. It may sound odd, but I believe rock energy is palpable—I have turned away certain rocks if they do not seem "comfortable" in a garden.

Plant your rocks as you would your flowers, and at least one-quarter of a rock should be buried. Through careful selection and placement of solid, natural rocks you can create a garden that helps us view Nature—and our time with her—a little differently. As Lily Tomlin said, "For fast acting relief, slow down." Rocks remind us to slow down.

Above: The dark pink, candelabra-like flowers of Japanese primrose (*Primula japonica*) thrive in wet, shady spaces in the landscape. These blooms are held 12 to 18 inches above the lettuce-like foliage and look wonderful when they flower in mid-May. They are especially vibrant when contrasted with ferns and large rocks or along streams. They are hardy in zones 4–8. I took this photo at the Elisabeth C. Miller Botanical Garden in Seattle, Washington.

Right: Graceful Diamond Frost® euphorbia (*Euphorbia* Diamond Frost®) sports small, airy, white flowers that bloom nonstop from spring through September. This drought-tolerant annual thrives in sun and partial shade. It stands 12 to 18 inches high. Excellent against mossy rocks, as shown here. It's deer resistant, too.

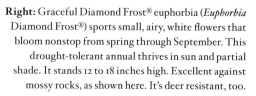

46. THE SECRET LIFE OF FLOWERS

I will never forget the day, in botany class at the University of Hawaii, when I realized that flowers were about one thing only—sex. I smiled to myself as the professor explained it all, and I thought, "Why, you little hussies!" After class, I walked through the campus and looked at every alluring flower with a new perspective.

The pollination ecologist Stephen Buchmann described it perfectly when he wrote, "flowers are literally living scented billboards that are advertising for sexual favors, whether those are from bees, flies, beetles, butterflies or us."

Flowers are simply asking to be pollinated in a most fabulous way. How clever. They dress up in all colors and shapes and release their perfume to attract the bees, butterflies, moths, and more. These flying pollinators, in turn, go for the sweet nectar within the flower and are then covered in pollen. They fly to the next flower, inadvertently spreading pollen as they go, which eventually leads to fruit and seeds.

Flowers, in fact, have developed sophisticated ways to attract pollinators beyond color, scent, and form. Recently, scientists have discovered that beach evening primrose (*Oenothera drummondii*) flowers can "hear" approaching bees and quickly make their nectar sweeter in response to the sound. Within three minutes of exposure to recordings of bees buzzing, sugar concentration in the plants increased from between 12 and 17 percent to 20 percent! The scientists theorize that bowl-shaped blossoms (such as those of beach evening primrose) act as a floral "satellite dish" that are eminently suitable for receiving and amplifying sound waves.

Flowers' colorful and fragrant "come hither" efforts are key to our survival. We depend on the secret life of flowers and their pollinators. Let's keep them all healthy and not do any harm to them.

Bees have less-than-perfect eyesight, so they see flowers only when they get reasonably close. This may be why scent is so useful to bees. Roses emit a marvelous fragrance to attract these bees.

47. THE BEST OF SILVER AND PURPLE (AND SOME PINK)

If you want to add an elegant, shimmery punch to a flower bed, plant some silvery or light gray foliage plants. Silver brightens the colors that surround it. It adds a modern touch to the landscape.

Blue and purple flowers work especially well with silvery or light gray leaves. Cool pink flowers also shine against silver foliage. Some of the best examples of silvery-leaved plants for flower gardens include dusty miller (*Jacobaea maritima*), artemisia, bugloss, licorice plant (*Helichrysum thianschanicum*), and Japanese painted fern (*Athyrium niponicum* var. *pictum*).

When you plant silver plants with purple and pink flowers check to see that they grow to similar heights. Likewise, do not plant drought-tolerant plants mixed with those that require lots of watering. Silver-leaved plants, as a whole, do not need too much watering, because light gray foliage is often an adaptation to dry conditions. Lastly, silver can dominate a bed with its sparkly look, so it is best used as an accent rather than as the main show.

Plants in the wormwood or *Artemisia* genus are a popular choice among gardeners. These light gray–leaved plants thrive in hot, full sun and poor soils. They are prized for the unusual shapes and color of their aromatic foliage. Check out varieties such as 'Powis Castle,' 'Silver Brocade,' 'Valerie Finnis,' and 'Silver Mound.' They can be cut back to keep within bounds, and all are deer resistant.

The many cultivars of Russian sage (*Perovskia* sp.), with their blue flowers, can be used as a silvery accent in a sunny garden. For a shade garden, try 'Moonshine' lungwort (*Pulmonaria* 'Moonshine'). Its leaves are completely silvered when mature, and a deep green edge makes the silvering pop.

The list of purple and pink flowers you can plant with silver plants includes purple and pink petunias, summer snapdragon, verbena, pansies, catmint, perennial salvia, annual salvia, sea holly, and more.

Top, left: The silvery, lacy foliage of dusty miller (*Jacobaea maritima*) makes a bright companion to purple summer snapdragon (*Angelonia*) and 'Titan Icy Pink' annual vinca. Dusty miller is fairly drought tolerant and is easy to grow. It is often grown as an annual but is hardy in zones 7–10. These three plants make a tough, heat-loving, deer-resistant flower combo.

Top, right: 'Silver Brocade' wormwood (*Artemisia stelleriana* 'Silver Brocade') has bright silvery white, deeply divided scalloped leaves. I planted this low, mounded plant next to the dainty lavender-blue flowers of the tender perennial laurentia (*Isotoma axillaris*). The pink-and-white blooms of 'Floral Lace' Violet Picotee dianthus (*Dianthus chinensis* × *barbatus*) add to the soft colors. Clip back 'Silver Brocade' hard in midsummer, when the stems begin to grow upright, in order to maintain a ground cover–like effect.

Bottom, left: Got shade? Try the silvery 'Jack Frost' Siberian bugloss (*Brunnera macrophylla* 'Jack Frost'), or one of the other similar cultivars. The frosty, heart-shaped leaves with elaborate green veins don't mind half-sun conditions. This perennial grows to 12 inches tall and is topped in spring by clusters of small blue flowers, similar in look to forget-me-nots. Shown here with purple pansies. A stunning combination in a May and June garden. Zones 3–7.

Bottom, right: 'Fragrant Delight' heliotrope (*Heliotropium arborescens* 'Fragrant Delight'), an easy-to-grow annual flower, is known for its intoxicating cherry-pie scent. The purple flowers and foliage with a silvery cast make a compelling silver-and-purple mix. Shown here with fuzzy foxtail fern (*Asparagus densiflorus* 'Myersii') in the background.

48. MORE IS MORE

The 20th-century architect Ludwig Mies van der Rohe famously said, "Less is more" when describing the design principles of minimalism. But when it comes to flower gardening many people follow the opposite philosophy of more is more. And why not? If we love the joy that flowers bring, then we cannot have too much of it. A flower garden overflowing with colors, scents, and textures is truly a floral embarrassment of riches.

Feel free to indulge the urge to stuff a flower bed or beds with an assortment of annual and perennial flowers and more. Go ahead—mix yellow marigolds with pink windflowers, purple alliums, fragrant heliotrope, and snow-white cosmos. Throw in some blue salvia and it becomes a veritable "floral stew" that simmers and blends its flavors all season long.

I must admit that the practice of more is more can be a little dangerous. Some people can take this to the extreme, and what was once a symphony of flowers can become a cacophony of colors, a crazy mishmash that disturbs rather than delights. So I add this advice: be thoughtful. "More" may become overwhelming, and so will be less appreciated. Even in flower gardening, you can have too much of a good thing.

When designing a garden, plant in layers. This will lessen any confusion. Have a background such as evergreen shrubs or trees in the distance. Plant flowers together but in large swaths or groups. Insert vertical accents like grasses or tall allium to punctuate the scene. And add flowers gradually rather than as an all-in-one-day adventure. Plant something, let it grow, and then if you fancy something more, add it later. The go-slow approach allows you to pop in something here and there throughout the season. Think of it as "a little more is a little more."

Top: A charming jumble of summer flowers is dominated by the airy white cosmos (*Cosmos bipinnatus*), an annual. Its widespreading and thin stems reach out to create an exuberant flowering mass. You can interplant flowers all together to create depth and joyfulness. Allow flowers to self-seed by leaving seed heads on the plants. Cosmos is a moderate reseeder.

Bottom, left: In early summer, this cottage-style flower garden is a mix of annuals and perennials. The spherical seed heads of the hybrid 'Globemaster' ornamental onion (*Allium* 'Globemaster') grow to 2½ feet high. They add a sculptural effect to a varied mix of flowers that include silver dusty miller, white cosmos, purple heliotrope, lavender ageratum, and pink wandflower. 'Globemaster' allium grows in zones 5–8.

Bottom, right: A mass of orange flowers of the perennial sneezeweed (*Helenium autumnale*) takes center stage in late summer and early fall. It is a native, sun-loving flower and likes lean soil to stay upright. Zones 4–8. It is growing in front of the deep magenta flowers of mountain fleece (*Persicaria amplexicaulis*). The blooms of airy tall verbena (*Verbena bonariensis*) insert some purple accents in the background. *Photo by Laura Hendrix McKillop.*

49. BRING FLOWERS INSIDE

"Flowers are, of all plants, the least menacing
and the most useless. Their sole purpose is to be
beautiful and to give pleasure."
—ELEANOR PERENYI, *GREEN THOUGHTS:
A WRITER IN THE GARDEN*

Flowers are useless? Of course not. They contain the reproductive organs of plants. Their beauty is a tool to lure pollinators. It is a timeless biological contrivance that flowers utilize so well! Flowers are evidence that looks, fragrance, and timing are a benefit in the reproductive arena. Beauty achieves its ends wonderfully when the goal is to attract suitors.

The attractiveness of flowers is their botanical calling card. And how lucky we are to be able to enjoy their efforts and also bring them indoors!

A glass jar filled with cut flowers on the kitchen counter becomes a natural jewel box of color and form. 'Cut and Come Again' zinnias, airy cosmos, 'Becky' Shasta daisies, and sweet baby's breath crowd each other for our attention and appreciation.

The visual appeal of flowers is more than a momentary pleasure. Beautiful things from Nature elevate and relax us. Henry David Thoreau, the 19th-century American philosopher, noted this in 1853: "All nature is doing her best

We now display more than the flower—this modern glass vase shows off the green stems almost as much as the flowers. Cut flower displays can celebrate seed heads and fruit as well.

each moment to make us well—she exists for no other end. Do not resist her."

And so, we grow flowers. Some of us may gather them to display their beauty indoors. And we share them at our happiest and saddest moments. Flowers project all kinds of meanings. In fact, a cryptic form of communication called floriography (the language of flowers) was developed in Turkey in the 16th century. Floriography uses flowers, and their meanings, to send secret messages.

A garden for cut flowers is perhaps the sweetest thing we can create—it allows us to share our flowers with others. Here are a few tips for gathering flowers for indoor displays:

- Cut the flowers early in the morning or evening. This is when their stems are filled with water and are sturdier.
- Make clean cuts on an angle to ensure greater water absorption.
- Place the flowers in warm water because it is more easily absorbed.
- Change the water frequently (every other day would be best).
- Make a fresh cut of the stems each time you change the water.

Top: Flowers stuffed in a small round container make a voluptuous display. Pink, lavender, and white with light green is a stunning color combination.

Bottom: The beauty of flowers is nowhere more appreciated than when they are placed in an attractive container. Here, my friend Mary used a black Sharpie pen to create a checkerboard pattern on plain white ceramic vases. It is an eye-catching counterpoint to the lisianthus and zinnias that she grows in her outstanding cut flower garden.

50. ONWARD AND UPWARD!

We don't often lift our eyes high to view flowers unless they are growing on trees. You can change this by training vining flowering plants up a tall obelisk, *tuteur*, or even a tall stick! One or more freestanding vertical structure festooned with flowers inserts a bit of drama to any landscape. Obelisks and *tuteurs* come in many heights and shapes, and they can be made from wood or metal. I placed a 6-foot-tall metal obelisk in a plant bed outside my dining room window and planted Jackman clematis (*Clematis jackmanii*) at its base—it blocks the view of the driveway when the large purple flowers appear each summer. During the holiday season, I twine several strings of white fairy lights around the obelisk for a festive touch.

What is the difference between an obelisk and *tuteur*? *Tuteurs* are freestanding, four sided, and pyramidal in shape. They have a stable base and taper toward the top. They originated in French traditional gardens. Obelisks are similar except they tend to be rectangular and may have a rounded top. Nowadays, the two names are often interchangeable. These climbing structures come in many sizes, and you can insert them in a planter or a garden bed. They are invaluable to gardeners with small outdoor spaces.

Some of my favorite flowering vines are morning glories, mandevillas, and honeysuckle. I particularly like the noninvasive common honeysuckle (*Lonicera periclymenum*), sometimes known as woodbine. It twines around overhead arbors, trellises, and even sturdy sticks and tree trunks. Its long-lasting flowers appear on new growth, and they emit a delicious scent. As an added bonus, you can use these versatile flowering vines as a lush seasonal privacy screen. Plant several small plants at the base of a well-built trellis and allow them to grow up and twine in and around the structure. Direct the vines' growth by gently moving the twining tendrils where you want them to go. Do this often when the growth is still soft and pliable.

Top, left: The compact clematis 'Amethyst Beauty' is a lovely flowered vine that grows well on a metal support. It sports 6-inch purple blossoms from early summer to late summer. The flower color changes from purple to lavender-blue as they age. It grows to 6 to 8 feet in zones 4–11. I planted this vine on a fence next to a gate so all who enter will see it.

Top, right: The pink-flowered 'Alice du Pont' mandevilla (*Mandevilla × amabilis* 'Alice du Pont') is a sun-loving vine that grows upward with the help of tendrils. It climbs up a *tuteur* easily, as shown here. Mandevilla is grown as an annual flower in northern climates but is a frost-tender perennial. It is hardy in zones 10–11. The flowers pop when contrasted with a dark green frame, as shown here.

Left: 'Goldflame' honeysuckle (*Lonicera × heckrottii* 'Goldflame') has a gorgeous mix of deep pink buds with golden-yellow, tubular flowers. They bloom throughout the summer with a sweet fragrance that you can smell on warm evenings. Semi-evergreen in milder climates. Not invasive, 10- to 15- feet-high twining vine, grows upward on trellises, arbors, or chain-link fences. Zones 5–9.

Left: Jewel tones are clear, vibrant colors that add sizzle to a garden. Here the bold yellow blooms of 'Safari Yellow' French marigold (*Tagetes patula* 'Safari Yellow') are planted next to Blue Horizon ageratum on the left and 'Bandana Cherry' lantana (*Lantana camara* 'Bandana Cherry') in the center. Also shown is 'Buddy Purple' globe amaranth (*Gomphrena globosa* 'Buddy Purple') and 'Serena Purple' summer snapdragon (*Angelonia angustifolia* 'Serena Purple'). The green foliage blends the varying colors nicely.

Bottom, left: I planted two shades of clear pink blooms of annual impatiens among the perennial stonecrop 'Autumn Joy' (*Hylotelephium telephium* 'Autumn Joy') for a restrained jewel-toned scene. The long-blooming stonecrop flowers will open to dark pink and slowly change to copper in fall. The bright colors of impatiens are muted by the shades of green and the variegated red twig dogwood (*Cornus alba* 'Elegantissima') behind them.

Bottom, right: Combined low-growing purple globe amaranth (*Gomphrena globosa*) with yellow-and-orange lantana for a jewel-toned rock garden planting. The light green sedum in the background helps to cool it off.

51. JEWEL TONES IN THE GARDEN

The term *jewel tones* sounds like a description of crystalline music, but it refers to color. Jewel tones are saturated colors that have the vibrancy of gemstones. Examples include emerald green, amethyst purple, ruby red, topaz yellow, sapphire blue, and turquoise. Gardens featuring bold jewel-toned flowers are exhilarating and, if done right, a theme garden of rich colors that sparkles like no other. But luxe tones must be used in moderation or the scene can become an overwhelming cacophony rather than a scintillating song.

Clear jewel-toned colors can be dazzling in an outdoor space. For a striking effect, use a variety of colorful blooms, from deep magenta to vibrant yellow, all mixed together. Or, instead of combining different bright hues, plant several species of flowers that sport the same deep color together. For this, try the magenta celosia 'Intenz' (*Celosia argentea* 'Intenz'), an easy-to-grow annual, interplanted with the sun-tolerant SunPatiens compact purple. They have the same magenta coloring. The flowers must be equally rich in color or one will overwhelm the other.

The most important tip for successful jewel-toned plantings is to add light and dark green foliage plants to cool it all down. Or insert some silvery foliage such as the hybrid 'Ghost' painted fern (*Athyrium* 'Ghost'), which grows in USDA hardiness zones 4–8. Try the spreading, tender perennial, variegated licorice plant (*Helichrysum petiolare* 'Licorice Splash') to set off the other colors.

The subdued, late-season light at the end of summer and into autumn enhances these sparkling colors. The vivid colors seem to shine more brightly then. For example, in late summer the marvelous bright colors of late-blooming dahlias can be matched with the light green foliage of sedum 'Angelina' (*Sedum rupestre* 'Angelina') and the low-growing globe amaranth 'Purple Gnome' (*Gomphrena globosa* 'Purple Gnome'), an annual. This floral mix is an eyepopper, for sure.

A jewel-tone theme can also apply to metallic planters, as shown here. (This was at Walt Disney World's annual Epcot International Flower & Garden Festival.) The bright blue planter is toned down by the soft pewter leaves of 'Silver Falls' dichondra (*Dichondra argentea* 'Silver Falls'), a vigorous plant with trailing stems. Zones 8–10.

52. SHORT, LOW GROWERS GRAB THE EYE

Up in front! The flowers or foliage that edge the front of a plant bed complete the display. Like a cuff on a shirt sleeve, low-growing flowers finish a planting nicely. The flowers at your feet—or at the front of a raised bed—are the important first layer in a tiered planting.

A colorful edge acts as an outline of a flower bed. The low-growing blossoms define the shape of the bed and make it readily visible. They call attention to the display. A garden design tip: use compact blue and purple flowers, such as blue ageratum or purple calibrachoa, as edging plants. These two colors are "recessive" and need to be in front to be noticed, otherwise the brighter colors will overpower them.

Low-growing foliage plants such as lilyturf (*Liriope*) or sedge (*Carex*) are often used in the front of a border, but there are some wonderful blooming flowers that are perfect for edging. I like zinnia 'Profusion,' in all its many colors, in the front of a plant bed. This annual flower grows just 12 to 15 inches high and wide, and it is covered with beautiful blooms all summer into fall. It's a carefree, vigorous choice for edging. I also like the ground-hugging flower candytuft (*Iberis sempervirens*), a perennial spring bloomer that is often used as a white-flowering ground cover along pathways. It is suitable for USDA hardiness zones 4–8. And a beautiful spreader is the perennial Serbian bellflower (*Campanula poscharskyana*). It bears starry lavender-blue, long-blooming flowers in late spring. Plant this perennial where it can spill over walls for a show of color. It does well in moderately rich, well-drained slopes where the 2-feet-long stems can trail. It is suitable for USDA hardiness zones 3–7.

When you plant or seed flowers as a first layer in your flower bed, set them back from the flower bed edge. This allows room for them to grow without spreading out beyond the bed. This is the reason why flower beds should be wider than you think—a wide bed allows plants room to grow.

Calibrachoa are small, petunia-like flowers that grow low and wide. They can trail up to 30 inches. They are annuals that bloom all season and, best of all, do not need deadheading. They love sun but will grow almost as well in partial shade. It attracts hummingbirds. Hardy in zones 9–11. This beautiful flower looks great in front of yellow Japanese forest grass (*Hakonechloa macra* 'Aureola').

Left: The mounded habit and snowy white flowers of candytuft (*Iberis sempervirens*), a perennial, light up the front of a garden in May. A popular cultivar is 'Purity,' which is densely growing to 10 inches in height. A great plant for attracting bees and butterflies, it likes dry, well-drained soil. Shear back one-third to one-half of the top growth just after flowering to promote a fall rebloom.

Right: 'Illusion Emerald Lace' sweet potato vine (*Ipomoea batatas* 'Illusion Emerald Lace') adds a chartreuse edge to any flower bed. It is a tender perennial grown as an annual foliage plant. It is heat tolerant and grows 6 to 10 inches high, spreading up to 30 inches. It can overgrow its bounds, but you can trim it at any time. It likes full-sun to part-shade locations. Hardy in zones 10–11.

White wax begonias, an annual, are a traditional low-growing edging flower. They keep flowering strong into the fall, as seen here.

53. NATURE'S TIME

A flower garden can teach us about time and how it works. Anyone who has lost themselves working in a garden knows intuitively about the elasticity of time. It ebbs and flows as we "lose track of time." This is Nature's time. It differs markedly from our human-centric mechanical time.

Mechanical time is the clock ticking. It is rigid and unyielding. Days are broken up into hours, minutes, seconds, milliseconds. Mechanical time puts constant pressure on our lives and makes us forget about the things that really matter.

Meister Eckhart, the 14th-century German Christian mystic, derided mechanical time as an obstacle in our lives: "Time is what keeps the light from reaching us. There is no greater obstacle to God than time: and not only time but temporalities, not only temporal things but temporal affections, not only temporal affections but the very taint and smell of time."

Nature's time, on the other hand, is made up of fits and starts. It is the unfolding of a flower, smooth and rhythmic; it is the torrent rush of rain in a summer squall. It is as eternal as a granite boulder and as fleeting as a snowflake on a sunny winter day.

Einstein explained that our dualistic reality is a blend of space and time. His scientific premise is echoed in the well-known phrase of American author Ram Dass: "Be here now." Gardens can help us do just that. We watch the annual unfurling of leaves and the bursting of buds, the ripening of berries. And we hear the familiar crunch of autumn leaves underfoot.

Nature's time needs no watches to measure it. The sun's rays and the moon's waxing and waning are its keepers. The flowers that bloom through the year are its sentinels.

Flowers need no watches to tell time—they follow Nature's rhythmic time. Here, an elegant deep purple lisianthus blossom blends beautifully with the spires of Delphinium's sky-blue flowers. This elegant perennial adds a beautiful vertical accent to any garden. It is known for its range of blue flowers. It prefers alkaline soil. After blooming in spring, cut back to 3 inches tall, add some compost, and you will get another round of blooms later in the year. Deer and rabbit resistant. Does not fare well in hot, dry weather. Zones 3–7.

An armillary sphere is one of the oldest astronomical instruments in the world. They are now usually used as a sundial. The armillary sundial is an open sphere circled by a ring with a gnomon in the shape of an arrow. It is set upon a tall base. As the sun travels across the sky, the gnomon casts a shadow onto the base surface that indicates the hour. I placed this in a flower garden I created for a dear client and friend.

Up until the early 19th century, sundials were a main instrument people used to tell time. A sundial tracks the position of the sun and the shadows fall on the general hour marker on its face. When positioning a sundial, align it to true north. Use a compass app on your cell phone to locate the direction of north. I set this small sundial in a flower garden. *Photo by Laura Hendrix McKillop.*

54. COLOR ECHOING

I use a technique called color echoing when I plant up mixed flower borders. It means repeating or spreading out the same color throughout the plant bed. It is very much like making a painting by repeating a color in various parts of the canvas. This color echo carries the eye around the entire picture. Likewise, it is a simple garden design technique that ties an outdoor space together. One color weaves through a landscape via the use of flowers, ornament, foliage, and even furniture.

In gardening, it can mean using the same flowering plant in different parts of a bed or using different flowering plants that have the same general color blooms. An example of the first technique is to plant a group of flowers in one part of a garden bed and another group on the other side of the bed. Hot pink New Guinea impatiens (*Impatiens hawkeri*) are a terrific choice. Alternatively, you can stagger the same impatiens plants randomly around the bed in a mosaic-type layout.

As they grow, they will make a beautiful tapestry of color.

Another color-echoing technique is to plant different plants with the same color. For example, plant white tuberous begonias in a bed and echo it with the white-and-green foliage of Swedish ivy, the airy white blooms of Diamond Frost® euphorbia, and the stately white of angelonia. The color ties them together even though they are all strikingly different. Scatter them around the plant bed.

Color echoing can be used with bold-colored flowers such as yellow marigolds or deep magenta rose campion (*Lychnis coronaria* 'Atrosanguinea'), a time-honored perennial. Color echoing is also effective with softer flower colors, because pastels are less dominant and blend colors together easily. You can also repeat foliage colors through a bed. No matter which colors you choose, echoing leads your eye around the entire scene and creates a sweeping harmony.

Pink is echoed around this rocky slope by the mauve-pink flowers of the dependable perennial 'Autumn Joy' stonecrop (*Hylotelephium telephium* 'Autumn Joy'). In this garden, I trim back the new growth of the stonecrop plants by half in June to keep them from growing too tall and then flopping over when in bloom. Do not trim after July 4. The other pink flowers are the dark-leaved annual pink begonias. In front, the grassy Bowles golden sedge (*Carex elata* 'Aurea') softens the edge. The dark leaves and yellow grass insert subtle contrasts. Flower garden design is part experimentation, or as I like to say, "planned accidents."

This long plant bed contains dwarf red impatiens (*Impatiens walleriana*), a tender perennial that is grown as an annual in cool climates. It has green, glossy leaves and grows to 8 to 10 inches tall and wide. It is easy to grow but can be afflicted with impatiens downy mildew, which kills the plants. Here, I echoed the flower bed with a planter containing a hybrid begonia with the same color blossom.

Left: The large gray-green fuzzy leaves of 'Helen von Stein' lamb's ear (*Stachys byzantina* 'Helen von Stein') make notable companions to the perennial 'Moonbeam' coreopsis (*Coreopsis verticillata* 'Moonbeam') and its lemon-yellow, dainty flowers. I planted this as a yellow and silver flower bed and included the annual 'Safari Yellow' French marigold. Lamb's ear can be grown in perennial flower gardens, as a ground cover, or as edging along walkways.

Below: I placed a pot of flowers within a bed of low-growing lamb's ear, possibly the 'Silver Carpet' variety. The gray, felty foliage makes a vivid contrast to the annual Superbells® 'Lemon Slice' calibrachoa, with its yellow flowers sporting a white pinwheel pattern from late spring to the first frost. And the pink Supertunia® 'Raspberry Blast' (*Petunia × hybrida* Supertunia® 'Raspberry Blast') adds a punch with its trumpet-shaped flowers with raspberry markings. No deadheading required!

55. INSERT SOME SOFT LAMB'S EAR

"With few exceptions . . . it is the memory of tactile experiences that enable us to appreciate texture."
—EDWARD T. HALL, *THE HIDDEN DIMENSION*

Texture, the way plants feel to the touch, is what makes them so memorable. Beautiful colors and scents may enthrall us, but we remember the way the leaves feel more than anything. That is why I suggest you insert some soft lamb's ear (*Stachys byzantina*) alongside your flowers. This low-growing perennial lives up to its name with thick, velvety foliage that adds a striking greenish-gray color to a garden bed. It sports 6- to 12-inch-tall spikes of small, bright, purplish pink flowers that bees and hummingbirds love in early summer. Some gardeners enjoy the flower spikes, but others cut them off as they emerge to promote the alluring foliage. Deer and rabbits do not eat lamb's ear. It is suitable for USDA hardiness zones 4–8.

Lamb's ear is native to Turkey, Iraq, and Iran (thus the species name *byzantina*), and it prefers full sun but may need light shade in warmer areas.

These adaptable plants thrive in well-drained soil and do not like wet conditions. They may rot in hot, humid areas. When crushed or cut, the leaves produce a fruity fragrance. This is a fun and easy-to-grow plant for children's gardens—no one can resist touching the fuzzy leaves.

A variety of lamb's ear that I suggest planting is 'Helen von Stein' (*Stachys byzantine* 'Helen von Stein'). It is also called Big Ears. It is a mounding plant, growing 8 inches tall, and rarely flowers. It does not reseed, which is why it is a good substitute for the common lamb's ear that can spread. Another great variety is the low-growing 'Silver Carpet' lamb's ear (*Stachys byzantina* 'Silver Carpet'), known for its attractive silvery green leaves. It does not bloom and grows 4 to 6 inches tall with a spread of 18 to 30 inches wide. 'Silver Carpet' makes a wonderful gray-leaved ground cover for areas with dry shade and poor soils.

56. GARDENING | WRITING

Is gardening like writing? I think so. This is what Carl Lennertz wrote in his blog, *Publishing Insider*:

> Every 5 years or so, I get a truckload of topsoil dropped off so I can elevate a corner of the yard or start a new flower bed. And it occurred to me, sleepily, that the sound of a shovel going into dirt is one of the most satisfying, tangible sounds, of all. The shoosh of metal on dirt, then the creation of something new. And then it hit me that writing was like that, too. The sound of writing, the sense of building something, measurable bit by bit, and most of all, the going back and reshaping and redoing.

I wholeheartedly agree. There is nothing more satisfying than seeing a garden emerge and grow after much labor and effort. I share Lennertz's simple pleasure of digging and planting—although I do it with a professional's sense of urgency to complete a project on time. But still, the "shoosh" of a shovel is a comfortable sound, like an old friend's voice or rain on the roof.

The shovel and rake are my comrades in arms just like the words that flow onto a page. In my case, each calls up the other. I cannot put down the shovel nor can I stop the words that seem to tumble out like ½-inch gravel around a subsurface drainage pipe (Ha!).

Gardening is indeed like writing. Weeding, cultivating, and enhancing are tasks that they share. If you neglect any of these steps, the result will suffer. Flowery prose must be pruned. Overstuffed plant beds must be edited.

I agree with Mr. Lennertz's notion that writing and gardening are quite similar—reshaping and redoing, both the earth and the words. It is the "building something, measurable bit by bit" that offers so much enjoyment.

A stand of perennial David's Chinese astilbe (*Astilbe chinensis* var. *davidii*) sends up lilac-purple flowers in July–August. The slightly wild look melds into the pond view beyond. These deer-resistant flowers prefer shade or partial sun. They need soil that is well drained and rich in organic material. David's Chinese astilbe grows to 4 feet tall and spreads vigorously, which is great for naturalizing a space. It is perfect for woodland gardens and shaded borders. Leave the seed heads standing for interest in winter. This is at the Berkshire Botanical Garden in Stockbridge, Massachusetts.

57. LET THE LAWN GO AND THE FLOWERS COME BACK

An estimated 80 percent of American households have a turfgrass lawn—that's a lot of fertilizer, fungicide, and afternoons spent mowing grass. And it eats up a lot of water. Why not let your lawn go natural? It would help the environment and free up some time for you to do other things in the garden. So let the lawn go and let the flowers come back!

Want more encouragement? The chemicals that you apply to the lawn reduce the populations of microbes, earthworms, and fungi that maintain fertility and the health of the soil. Rain washes the lawn pesticides, herbicides, and fertilizers into local streams, polluting our waterways and harming the amphibians that live there. This sad situation must be changed.

A more diverse natural landscape will bring songbirds, pollinators, and wildflowers into your yard. A good way to encourage wildflowers in your garden is to leave a part of the lawn to its own devices during spring and summer, with a few mowings. Add some wildflower seeds. The lawn will become a diverse palette of flowering plants that support bees and other wildlife. You may find dandelions, violets, white clover, creeping Charlie (ground ivy), speedwell, and buttercups showing up. These low-growing vigorous "weed" plants will endure shade, some mowing, and light foot traffic. And they will be visited by pollinators! White clover, for example, is a lawn "weed" that is a summertime flower especially loved by honeybees. Clover has edible leaves and flowers and is also a nitrogen fixer. It assimilates nitrogen from the atmosphere.

To go natural, start by mowing your lawn less frequently. Allow the dandelions to bloom. Do not apply chemical fertilizer. And do not apply pesticides—many invertebrates control pests, pollinate flowering plants, and provide food for other wildlife. Scatter a wildflower and grass seed mix that is blended for your region. This will introduce wildflowers to your natural lawn. An online resource for this is the Xerces Society (www.xerces.org), a nonprofit organization. They sell a variety of pollinator conservation seed mixes.

Clover, dandelions, and violets have all taken root in this natural lawn. The flowers appear in early spring. Wild violets (*Viola* spp.) can become quite aggressive in the lawn and are hard to eradicate. But the yellow, purple, or white violet flowers feed early and efficient pollinators, such as the native blue orchard bee. Hardy in zones 4–9.

58. BACKDROPS MAKE FLOWERS "POP"

Flowers really "pop" if you have a backdrop. Without something to stop the eye, a flower planting can look lonely and stark, like a circle of marigolds or perennial baptisia growing in the middle of an open lawn. Backgrounds provide a boundary or "sense of place" by enclosing the view. It can be a physical screen such as a fence, a shrub, a hedge, or a wall. A tall shrub with dark red foliage, such as 'Royal Purple' smokebush, makes a great backdrop, because the deep color sets off the color of the flowers in front of it.

The backdrop does not have to be close. It may be a distant view where a meadow, slope, or lawn rises, offering a faraway uphill background, as in an impressionist painting. This is called a high horizontal line. The lower part of the view is a flower bed, while the upper view is a hillside behind and above the blossoms. It is an effective way to utilize a slope.

A stone wall makes a great solid backdrop for flowers. The natural stones offer a textured contrast to the color and form of the flowers. If you have a wall, consider adding a flower bed in front of a portion of it. A tall, sunny stone wall will radiate heat back to the flowers, so plant heat-tolerant flowers like perennial yarrow, sedum, or blanket flower (*Gaillardia*) to take advantage of that microclimate.

One other possibility for a floral backdrop is an open, rustic trellis fence with vines growing up and around the rough posts. The trellis can be made from weathered, free-form branches that span the distance between several equally spaced wood posts. Train climbing vines such as Dutchman's pipe (*Aristolochia macrophylla*) on the trellis to serve as a green backdrop to a flower bed.

Top, left: A solid white fence and gate create a beautiful backdrop for black-eyed Susans, coneflowers, and 'Autumn Joy' sedum. The climbing morning glory vine by the gate adds to the lushness of the scene. You may choose to paint the fence a dark color such as a deep black-green if you want to add some drama to the garden.

Top, right: Red daylilies (*Hemerocallis* spp.) with their bright red trumpets and contrasting lemon-yellow throat bloom in midsummer in front of a dark-leaved background of a 'Royal Purple' smokebush. Varieties of smokebush have deep burgundy to purplish leaves. Daylilies grow from thick, tuberous roots that are easily divided.

Bottom: Large, yellow Mexican marigolds (*Tagetes erecta*) stand out against a dark green, ivy-covered wall. This is an excellent choice for summer-long color in a sunny location.

59. "MALIGNANT" MAGENTA

When it comes to color in the garden, people have strong opinions. Their likes and dislikes are on a visceral level, and for that reason their opinions are hard to change. Some people hate orange, while others dislike purple or a certain shade of purple. In fact, for many years there was a taboo among some gardeners against planting magenta flowers, those with a strong purplish-pink hue. This can be traced back to the 19th-century British horticulturist Gertrude Jekyll, an influential garden writer and tastemaker. In 1899, she saddled magenta with the descriptive *malignant*. From that time forward "malignant magenta" was not seen in fashionable gardens. Magenta did have its defenders, such as the early 20th-century American garden writer Louise Beebe Wilder, who wrote the book, *Color in My Garden*, in 1918. She celebrated the maligned color, describing it as "the imperial scarf of magenta" on summer phlox.

Why does magenta elicit such strong opinions? Those who hate it call it garish and harsh. They note that magenta is not really a color because it is not found naturally in Nature. This is true. The color magenta was developed in the mid-19th century as a synthetic aniline dye. It was named after the 1859 Battle of Magenta in Italy. The popularity of this seemingly unnatural color during that time was enormous. Everyone wore, and was surrounded by, magenta and its various shades. Unfortunately, the manufacturing of magenta-based dyes resulted in a poisonous byproduct, an arsenic compound called London purple. Soon the new color, magenta, was associated with toxic materials; hence, the descriptive term *malignant* was affixed to magenta.

This aversion to magenta continues today. Its disfavor even appeared in a popular 20th-century television sitcom, *The Golden Girls*, when one of the characters, Blanche Devereaux, says, "And I hate the color magenta. . . . No way to really explain it but, fortunately between friends you don't have to." And so it goes with magenta . . .

Bold and bright, zinnias come in a variety of intense colors, including magenta. Here, a summer border of regal, heat-tolerant zinnias on long, strong stems add pizazz to a roadside garden. A popular annual flower, they are easy to grow from seed and make an ideal cut flower.

Above: A wide swath of 'Fatal Attraction' coneflower (*Echinacea purpurea* 'Fatal Attraction') shows off magenta flowers with large central cones. This is a hybrid of the US native, purple coneflower, from Dutch breeder and garden designer, Piet Oudolf. 'Fatal Attraction' is a compact purple coneflower that has slightly upturned magenta purple rays that do not droop. Flowers top black stems. It grows over 2 feet tall and attracts bees, butterflies, and birds to a garden. Flowers bloom from June to early September. Zones 4–9. *Photo by Laura Hendrix McKillop.*

Left: The esteemed American garden writer Louise Beebe Wilder wrote in defense of her "beloved magenta blossoms" and praised the magenta summer phlox "that stoops to bind the dusty roadside." Here, magenta-colored flowers of garden phlox (*Phlox paniculata*) hold their own against a robin's egg–blue picnic table. The bright summer sun seems to soften the purplish-pink hue. Needs full sun. Zones 4–8.

60. FUN WITH UMBELS

I love umbels! The word *umbel* describes the radial disks of flowers seen in anise, dill, fennel, angelica, celery, and flat-leaf parsley among others. It is derived from the Latin word *umbella*, meaning "parasol." This is fitting since the lacy flowers look like an umbrella, having short flower stalks holding clusters of many tiny individual flowers that radiate out from a common central point. Umbel flowers range from flat topped, like Queen Anne's lace (*Daucus carota*), to almost spherical, like chives. They are found on plants in the aromatic plant family *Apiaceae*. As the name suggests (*apis* is the Latin word for bee), these flowers are filled with lots of pollen and nectar, and they are a magnet for beneficial insects such as small native bees, lacewings, hoverflies, and parasitic wasps.

The allure of umbel flowers is in their intricate detail and delicacy, such as in the white Queen Anne's lace that appears in masses along roadsides in summer. Its flowers are visited by native pollinators, and its foliage feeds the caterpillars of black swallowtail butterflies.

Umbels are a little on the wild side, and when placed in a garden setting, elevate it to an enchanted, lighthearted scene. This is particularly true of the striking, spherical flowers of ornamental onion (*Allium* spp.) and the dramatic crimson flowers of the 5- to 6-feet-tall Korean angelica (*Angelica gigas*) that bloom in August through September. Want to spice up a moist, deer-resistant garden with an umbel? Add the deep mauve-pink, pincushion-like blooms of the perennial 'Star of Beauty' masterwort (*Astrantia major* 'Star of Beauty'). The flowers explode above white bracts (leaves) that are tipped in burgundy. Also try the clear pink flowers of 'Roma' masterwort (*Astrantia major* 'Roma'). As a bonus,

the bracts of astrantia will remain attractive after flowers fade. It is suitable for USDA hardiness zones 4–7.

A word of warning: umbels are basically like carrots, meaning they have a taproot. The exception to this is astrantia. Dividing these plants is difficult, but collecting the seed is easy. Make sure to add some umbelliferous flowers to your landscape. You will enjoy it and so will the pollinators.

Top, left: Queen Anne's lace (*Daucus carota*) is a wildflower that blooms in the heat of summer. Its delicate, white, disk-shaped flowers float atop 3-foot stems and can be seen growing along roadsides. It is drought tolerant and can grow in infertile soils. Often referred to as wild carrot, it is a biennial—completing its life cycle in two years. During the first year, the plant produces a rosette of green leaves; and in the second year, Queen Anne's lace produces the compound, umbel-shaped flowers we all enjoy. After the flowers are pollinated, they curl upward to protect the maturing seeds.

Top, right: Bronze fennel (*Foeniculum vulgare* Purpureum) has ferny, dark purple-brown foliage with stalks of golden floral umbels. Beneficial insects like bees and hoverflies love this plant. It's a host plant for swallowtail butterflies. Prefers a sunny spot and moist, well-drained soil but will tolerate drought. Bronze fennel will freely self-seed. Plant with tall verbena (*Verbena bonariensis*) for a show. Zones 5–9.

Bottom, left: 'Dara,' a cultivar of Queen Anne's lace (*Daucus carota* 'Dara'), is an elegant umbellifer with finely divided green foliage and doily-like flowers in shades of dark purple, pink, or white. The attractive 3- to 5-inch lacy umbels sit atop strong, upright stems. 'Dara' Queen Anne's lace self-seeds readily. A great cut flower that lasts long in bouquets.

Bottom, right: Ornamental onion (*Allium* spp.) flowers are spherical umbels. Their seed heads look like little fireworks atop leafless flower stems rising above the foliage. The bees and butterflies love them, but deer avoid them! Here, an ornamental onion variety has been interplanted with the purple flowers of another deer-resistant flower, spiderwort (*Tradescantia virginiana*).

61. TIPS FOR LAYERING WITH FLOWERS

Layering with flowers, planting a little here and a little there, is a delightful activity. Of course it requires some planning, but it is so satisfying! Layer or repeat dominant shapes and colors within the plant bed. Use many mounded flowering plants because low, rounded forms are easy on the eyes and allow you to pay more attention to the entire scene. Plant some mounded perennial plants like the compact 'Kim's Knee High' coneflower. Also, intersperse medium-height sedums, coreopsis, yarrow, aster, and summer-blooming 'Snowcap' Shasta daisy in the garden bed, keeping color and bloom time in mind.

To add to the layering of shapes, make sure spring, summer, and fall bloomers are spread around to keep the show going. The plants coming into bloom will cover those that have already flowered, like summer daylilies hiding the tulip foliage or fall asters covering spent Shasta daisies.

Add a few spiky flowering plants to the mounded forms to insert drama. Try speedwell, tall astilbe, and foxglove. I even use yucca for a stiff pointed-leaf accent. Be careful to limit the number of tall dramatic flowers you use. Spikes like attention and can dominate a little too much.

Then plant soft, wavy grasses for contrast. I prefer short grasses in the front of the bed—they make a nice transition with taller plants. Grassy plants such as sedge, fountain grass (*Pennisetum* spp.), and prairie dropseed (*Sporobolus heterolepis*) connote a certain amount of wildness.

Of course, taller plants go in the back of the scene. But sometimes you can place a tall flower in the center of the bed just to mix up the predictable tiered look. Pop in a group of tall ornamental onion (*Allium* spp.) to add height in late spring and summer.

Top: Here, low-growing lemon-yellow 'Moonbeam' coreopsis (*Coreopsis verticillata* 'Moonbeam'), white Angelonia, and 'Ice Dance' Japanese sedge (*Carex morrowii* 'Ice Dance') are backed by a large swath of 'Autumn Joy' sedum (*Hylotelephium telephium* 'Autumn Joy') and the vibrant blooms of 'Goldsturm' black-eyed Susan (*Rudbeckia fulgida* var. *sullivantii* 'Goldsturm').

Bottom: I layered tall verbena (*Verbena bonariensis*), an annual, with perennial dark blue salvia and perennial lavender catmint, up front. This is a great deer-resistant combination that pollinators love.

62. THE ELUSIVE BLUE FLOWER

"I love blue more than any other color. I am inordinately attracted to any blue substance: to minerals like turquoise and lapis lazuli, to sapphires and aquamarines . . . and to a blue flower whether or not it has any other merit."
—ELEANOR PERENYI

The great American garden writer Eleanor Perenyi expressed what we all feel, that blue is a very appealing color. It is the most popular color in the world. Although most flowers come in hues of yellow, orange, red, and purple, there are relatively few blue flowers. Why? There is no true blue pigment in plants. The plants actually alter red anthocyanin pigments to make blue. These modifications, made naturally by the plants, combine with reflected light to create shades of blue. And so we have glorious blue flowers such as delphiniums, globe thistles, ageratums, irises, agapanthus, morning glories, and cornflowers, among others.

Not all blues are true blue. Often, what appears to be purple or violet flowers are labeled as blue. Blue-purple is a more common flower color than a clear blue. For this reason, we accept purple into the blue flower mix.

If true blue flowers are your goal, try deer-resistant gentian 'True Blue' (*Gentiana* 'True Blue'). Another perennial that has vivid blue flowers is 'Crater Lake Blue' speedwell (*Veronica austriaca* 'Crater Lake Blue'). Its much shorter cousin, 'Georgia Blue' creeping speedwell (*Veronica peduncularis* 'Georgia Blue'), is a low-growing, evergreen ground cover with rich blue flowers in early to late spring. And there is the tender perennial 'Blue My Mind' dwarf morning glory (*Evolvulus* 'Blue My Mind'), with nonstop, bright blue flowers that cover a spreading, silvery green plant. Grown as an annual and flowering from late spring until frost, it is great in planters. It is suitable for USDA hardiness zones 9–11.

To help blue flowers stand out, plant them in a large group. This works well because blue is a recessive color. In other words, unlike bold red, yellow, or white flowers, blue flowers need to be in front or in a large grouping to be noticed. An effective way to mass blue-purple flowers is to plant a wide swath of them winding through a flower bed or ground cover bed. Try curving a wide line of annual or perennial blue salvia. This "river of blue" directs the eye in a most dramatic way.

Bottom, left: The genus *Salvia* includes some of the clearest blue blossoms. The annual mealycup sage (*Salvia farinacea*) is a true performer in the summer and fall garden with strong upright flower spikes. Here, the cultivar 'Victoria Blue' (*Salvia farinacea* 'Victoria Blue') blooms in a corner planting bed. The blue color becomes deeper in cool weather, as shown here. Seldom damaged by deer. *Photo by Laura Hendrix McKillop.*

Bottom, right: The beautiful sky-blue flowers of trailing annual lobelia (*Lobelia erinus*), shown here in a planter set atop a tree stump chair, is a standout.

Top, left: The Himalayan blue poppy (*Meconopsis betonicifolia*) is known for its large, silky, sky-blue flowers. The variety shown is *Meconopsis* Lingholm, a perennial that has rich blue flowers up to 4 inches wide on 3-foot-high stalks and blooms from late spring to early summer. The blue poppy derives its blue color from the pigment delphinidin, which also gives blue hues to *Viola* and *Delphinium*. It does best in a rich soil that does not dry out. I took this photo at the Rhododendron Species Botanical Garden in Federal Way, Washington, which has a delightful Meconopsis Meadow containing several hundred specimens! Zones 3–9.

Top, right: *Tradescantia* 'Blue & Gold,' commonly known as 'Blue & Gold' spiderwort or 'Sweet Kate,' is a remarkable perennial. It has bright chartreuse-yellow grassy foliage, bejeweled with rich gentian-blue triangular flowers. It will flower all summer if old blooms are removed. It is easy to grow in many soil types, even wet sites. Attractive to butterflies. Full sun to partial shade. Zones 3–9.

Above: As you walk across the Bridge of Flowers, you can catch a glimpse of the Deerfield River beyond the gorgeous array of annual and perennial blooms. This photo was taken in early July when the seed heads of ornamental onion (*Allium* spp.) stand above the purple spikes of gayfeather (*Liatris spicata*), red poppies, and the small white blossoms of feverfew (*Tanacetum parthenium*). *Photo by Michele Fitzgerald.*

Opposite page: Red poppies grow within a mix of blue and lavender cornflowers (*Centaurea cyanus*) on the Bridge of Flowers. The extensive variety of flowers growing here ensures that something is always in bloom. This unique public space is another "must visit" for every garden lover. *Photo by Michele Fitzgerald.*

63. THE BRIDGE OF FLOWERS IN SHELBURNE FALLS, MASSACHUSETTS

What do you do with an old, defunct trolley bridge that has become an eyesore? You turn it into a one-of-a-kind flowering landmark! That is what The Shelburne Falls Area Women's Club in Massachusetts did almost 100 years ago. The bridge was built for trolleys to cross the Deerfield River in 1908. But the trolley railway went out of business in 1927 and it sat idle for several years. In 1929, with the bridge covered in weeds, local residents Antoinette and Walter Burnham came up with the idea of transforming the bridge into a garden. The community liked their idea, since the bridge carried a water main and could not be demolished. After 80 loads of topsoil were deposited on the bridge, and donated plants and flowers were installed, the concrete structure was reborn as the Bridge of Flowers.

Today, the 400-foot-long, five-arched concrete bridge is a flower-lover's dream. There are over 500 varieties of flowers, vines, and shrubs growing together. There is always something in bloom from April to October, beginning with violets and spring bulbs and ending with dahlias and chrysanthemums. The colorful flowers, some of which are rare or historical varieties, border both sides of a narrow walkway in the center of the bridge. Each flower type is labeled to satisfy the interest of visitors who come from all over the world.

In 1983, the Bridge of Flowers was completely renovated at a cost of a half-million dollars. Over 500 individuals, businesses, and organizations donated to the campaign. Every plant was removed from the bridge and was cared for in private gardens during the restoration. The Shelburne Falls Area Women's Club continues to sponsor and volunteer in weeding and caring for the plants each week, making sure the bridge garden is looking its best. Head gardener Carol DeLorenzo has overseen the garden for over 20 years and recently accepted the Bee Spaces pollinator award on behalf of the pollinator-friendly Bridge of Flowers.

For an extensive list of the flowers and shrubs you can expect to see on the awe-inspiring Bridge of Flowers, and their time of bloom, go to their website: www.bridgeofflowersmass.org. The Bridge of Flowers is open from April 1 through October 30.

64. ORANGE YOU GLAD YOU PLANTED ORANGE FLOWERS?

Orange flowers are bright and fiery. They insert an energetic punch to any garden. And orange does not lose its powerful presence and get washed out even on a bright summer afternoon. So then why do so many people say they "hate" orange? Maybe it is because orange has a boisterous personality that is not very calming. It is a little too brash to some garden lovers, like a loud person in a library. But you can use the radiance of orange to add a bit of warmth to a multicolored landscape. Carefully blending orange, and its softer tints, with other colors can win over even the most ardent anti-orange person.

To begin, try inserting a light-colored shade of orange to an outdoor space. The warm pink-orange tints of salmon, coral, and peach add a dreamy, soft edge to a garden. They are vibrant yet mellow. Dahlias come in these sensuous tones, as do tulips, astilbes, New Guinea impatiens, snapdragons, zinnias, and diascia. Add some blue in the form of violas, angelonia, baptisia, or catmint to the mix and the result is positively lovely.

Bright orange blooms work best in summer and early fall when the sun's rays are intense and complement this strong color. A wonderful orange perennial is Peruvian lily 'Indian Summer' (*Alstroemeria inticancha* 'Indian Summer'). Its red, yellow, and orange funnel-shaped flowers bloom from June to November. It is hardy in USDA hardiness zones 6–9. Alstroemeria does well planted in a container and makes a great cut flower.

You can mute the orange by pairing it with bronzy or burgundy foliage such as 'Marooned' coleus, 'Charmed Wine' oxalis, heuchera, 'Tropicanna' canna lilies, or shrubs like 'Summer Wine' ninebark.

Also try the dark, dusky orange shades of flowers like perennial yarrow. Look for varieties with tones that range from brick red to golden beige. They add a sultry look to a garden. Also look for chrysanthemums, dahlias, and coneflowers in similar hues. Pair them with cream-colored flowers.

This zinnia has twisted, shaggy salmon-pink petals that are curled at the tips. It looks like a dahlia. It is a "cactus style" zinnia called 'Señorita' (*Zinnia elegans* 'Señorita'). Its unique shape and soft shade of salmon-apricot steal the show every time! The showy blooms grow on strong 3-foot-tall stems. They make elegant cut flowers. Plant this sun-loving annual along with the purplish-blue flowers of anise hyssop (*Agastache foeniculum*). A vivid orange version of a cactus- or dahlia-type zinnia is Aztec. The spectacular blooms add a brilliant tangerine "wow" to any garden.

Top, left: Peruvian lilies are excellent as long-lasting cut flowers. These perennials grow from tubers and prefer well-drained soil. The cultivar shown is 'Indian Summer' (*Alstroemeria inticancha* 'Indian Summer'). It grows 26 to 30 inches high with sturdy stems. Deadheading will promote better blooms the following year. Simply grasp the dead flower stem and pull the entire stem out from the base of the plant. Needs sun to thrive. No staking required.

Top, right: The late-summer flowering 'Helena Red Shades' helenium (*Helenium autumnale* 'Helena Red Shades') is a cultivar of a native wildflower. Also called sneezeweed, it prefers full to partial sun and moist soils. 'Helena Red Shades' has long, blooming, coppery red flowers with eye-catching central cones that are full of pollen and nectar that attract bees and butterflies. Rusty brown seed clusters attract birds. Grows to 4 feet high. Pinch back in early summer to reduce height. Looks great with ornamental grasses, fall blooming asters, and Japanese anemones. Zones 3–9.

Left: 'Princess Irene' triumph tulip has unique orange blossoms with smoky purple flames. It is a sturdy, midspring bloomer with a warm scent. This orange beauty is a favorite at Holland's famous Keukenhof gardens. It can be planted in the ground or in planters. Plant tulip bulbs in the fall. Purple and violet flowers provide a wonderful contrast to orange, as shown here. Zones 3–7.

65. PIET OUDOLF'S GARDEN DESIGN TIPS

"My biggest inspiration is nature.
I do not want to copy it but to recreate the emotion."
—PIET OUDOLF

Garden design is not defined as an art form, but I think it should be. If there was ever a Picasso of garden design it is the Dutch plantsman, Piet Oudolf (pronounced Peet Ow-dolf). He is at the forefront of a naturalistic garden style known as the Dutch Wave. This style celebrates the disordered cycles of life and death in the landscape using perennial flowers and grasses. Plants flourish during the growing season, then the seed heads and brown stalks of fall and winter are left to remain until the following year. They are as visually important as the fresh new growth of spring or the abundant flowers of summer, and so they are not cut down. The garden becomes animated with an ever-changing wildness through the entire year.

Piet Oudolf carefully plans his perennial gardens, but he mimics the feeling of Nature with repeating colors and plant varieties. He divides the forms of flowers and seed heads into daisies, spires, buttons, globes, and more. It all blends into a flowing symphony of perennials and grasses. Here are a few Oudolf garden design tips:

- Plant hardy perennials that withstand harsh weather.
- Choose "structure" plants: sturdy, long-blooming perennials and grasses that can be cut down in early spring. Plant up to 70 percent of the garden with these and repeat them in large swaths, spaced around evenly. For example, Oudolf uses varieties of coneflowers (*Echinacea* spp.) as one of his structural plants.
- Plant the remaining 30 percent of the garden with filler plants that provide feathery or airy texture or foliage color. Intertwine them with the structural plants. Filler plants include certain grasses, iris, sedum, calamint, and mountain mint.
- Encourage plants to self-sow among themselves.
- Plan out successive blooms through the year. Predetermine the location of the spring flowers, followed by the summer and fall flowers.

Top: The summer flowers at Piet Oudolf's garden and nursery, Hummelo, in the Netherlands, include 'Fatal Attraction' coneflower, blue skullcap (*Scuttellaria incana*), orange helenium, and puffy joe-pye weed, on the right. *Photo by Laura Hendrix McKillop.*

Bottom, left: "And brown is also a color." This statement by Piet Oudolf reminds us to appreciate the full life cycle of flowers. Here, in his personal garden, Hummelo, in the Netherlands, the round seed heads of allium combine with airy grasses behind it. *Photo by Laura Hendrix McKillop.*

Bottom, right: Piet Oudolf says the real test of a garden isn't "how nicely it blooms but how beautifully it decomposes." He reminds us, with his gardens, that beauty is inherent in all the seasons.

66. LEARNING FROM MONET

"More than anything, I must have flowers, always, always."
—CLAUDE MONET

Claude Monet, the 19th-century French impressionist painter, is almost as famous for his garden in Giverny, France, as he is for his artwork. Monet's world-class landscape reveals that he was a skilled horticulturist and garden designer. Winding paths, ponds, rhododendrons, flowers, and of course his beloved waterlilies, delight the many visitors who flock to his floral haven 35 miles outside of Paris.

It took 20 years for Monet to transform an abandoned cider farm into a garden of his liking. He was its head designer and gardener. Interestingly, he specifically created garden scenes that he could paint. He dug a pond, planted waterlilies, and then painted them to great acclaim. This was far different from the painters of his time who simply painted the landscapes they found.

Taking a cue from Monet's suggestion in a flower bed—plant brightly colored flowers near the front of plant beds and more muted flowers in the background to create the illusion of depth.

Monet was obsessed by the beauty and color of flowers, and he stayed up to date on new varieties to try. He used flowers as if they were paint and played with color in innovative ways. For example, Monet experimented with blocks of single colors and collected blue-hued plants because this color is rare in Nature.

His unique color experimentation took place in the 38 "paint box" flower beds that he constructed. They served as smaller versions of the long flower beds found in the main garden. In these, Monet tried out new plants and unusual color, texture, and height combinations before committing to them and including them in his garden. He studied how the light through the day changed the colors.

This idea of a paint box flower bed can be modified to any size plot. Why not install a few small experimental beds for your own flower trials? When someone asks why you call it a paint box, explain that it began with Claude Monet, gardener extraordinaire.

One interesting aspect of Monet's garden in Giverny, France, is that the built features—shutters, benches, steps, porch, wisteria-draped footbridge, and even a rowboat—are painted an intriguing shade of green. Here, at the Phipps Conservatory and Botanical Gardens in Pittsburgh, Pennsylvania, they re-created Monet's green "Japanese bridge." The closest match to his special green is Benjamin Moore's Juniper. This was determined by the New York Botanical Garden using photo matching and consulting the experts at the Monet home.

> "To plant a garden is to believe in tomorrow."
> —AUDREY HEPBURN

———

THEMES FOR FLOWER GARDENS

———

We all love to pop a new plant into our garden or container. It speaks to us of possibility. This is especially true in spring when we go to the nursery or garden center and buy whatever looks good at the moment. We plant it up and say, "This will be great." But the moment passes, and it doesn't quite do the trick. What to do? Maybe it is time to choose a theme for your garden! It may sound odd, but having a general theme can help focus your gardening efforts. It can be something simple like a Wild Garden, or it can be more involved like a Blue and Yellow Garden. Just remember to follow the site's inherent qualities—you cannot create a dry, desert garden in a ferny hollow.

In order to choose a suitable theme, ask yourself some questions. For example, are you a private person or do you like to entertain people? What kind of environment appeals to you: cozy or elegant? Exciting or serene? Do you like airy, open spaces or more enclosed areas? Knowing this can help you think about which outdoor setting you want to create. Additionally, consider if you want a romantic garden, a woodland garden, or an outdoor area where you can attract as many kinds of birds and insects as possible. And of course, if you love a certain plant, such as dahlias, you may want to plant as many varieties as you can.

Once you choose a theme, you are free to indulge your creative energies. Themes like a Butterfly Garden or an English Cottage Garden can help you choose the plants, the garden accents, the colors, and even the outdoor furniture! It helps to establish a feeling and a look. These garden themes are catchy!

Flowers and flower gardening lend themselves well to theme gardens. For example, you can categorize herbaceous flowers by color and follow the theme of a Purple and Lime-Green Garden. Or you can choose flowers according to their smell and create a Fragrance Garden. You may decide on a seasonal theme and have a panoply of autumn-blooming flowers in a Fall Flower Delight Garden. The idea of a Bee-Friendly Garden should be in every garden, while a White Garden showcases a multitude of snowy blooms such as white zinnias, astilbes, Japanese anemones, and more. The possibilities are many, and the creativity that a theme garden may engender is great. You can be as artistic as you wish, while making things grow. As Liberty Hyde Bailey, known as America's Father of Modern Horticulture, wrote in his influential book, *The Holy Earth* (1915): "The proper caretaking of the earth lies not alone in maintaining its fertility or in safeguarding its products. The lines of beauty that appeal to the eye and the charm that satisfies the five senses are in our keeping."

The charm that satisfies our five senses can be found in a flower garden, and theme gardens can enhance that charm even more. We can create "lines of beauty," as Bailey called them, and take care of the earth, and its pollinators, at the same time. As he said, it is in our keeping.

How about a Blue and Orange Garden? These two colors are opposite, or complementary, on the color wheel, which means they create a high contrast. The bright orange helps the "shy" blue to stand out. Planting together flowers of complementary colors, like yellow and purple or red and green, adds visual excitement to your garden. Here, low-growing 'Blue Clips' bellflower (*Campanula carpatica* 'Blue Clips') blooms alongside deep orange daylilies in a raised bed planting. Both perennials bloom in midsummer and continue blooming for weeks.

Above: Catmint and daisies are two great perennial flowers for a meadow-style planting.

Top, right: The rosy pink flower heads of 'Millenium' ornamental onion (*Allium* 'Millenium') and the towering stems of tall verbena (*Verbena bonariensis*) are both stars of pollinator gardens, attracting bees and butterflies and more.

Bottom, right: Botanical gardens and other public gardens can offer some great planting ideas for your home landscape. The wonderful Harry P. Leu Gardens in Orlando, Florida, has a theme for that: an Idea Garden.

67. A DEER-RESISTANT FLOWER GARDEN

In my part of the world, deer are rampant. They walk the streets of my village, unafraid. They munch on our front yard and backyard plants like a free buffet. This sad situation can make a plant lover sigh with resignation. But—with a little knowledge—you can have a lovely flower garden that deer avoid, or at least, not chew on.

Once you start to look, you can find many perennial and annual flowers that deer rarely or seldom damage. I use the term *deer-resistant plant* rather than *deer-proof*, because you never really know what deer will choose to eat. A few of my favorite deer-resistant perennials include Japanese wind anemones, astilbe, catmint, lavender, salvia, ornamental onion, bleeding heart, and coreopsis. They can be planted along with deer-resistant annuals, grasses, and ferns to make quite a show.

You can grow almost any plant if you install a tall, protective deer fence or apply deer sprays on the plants to make them unpalatable. But, in my mind, it is far easier (and less costly) to choose plants that deer don't particularly like to eat. I note many deer-resistant flowers in this book. A great informative website source on deer-resistant plants is "Landscape Plants Rated by Deer Resistance," developed by Rutgers University (njaes.rutgers.edu/deer-resistant-plants). It rates all types of landscape plants that grow in New Jersey, and similar hardiness zones, in several deer-resistant categories, from Rarely Damaged to Frequently Severely Damaged.

Left: I created this overflowing flower border with an eye to deer resistance. The blue annual salvia, light pink annual vinca, dark pink lantana, and lavender-blue summer snapdragon are all deer resistant!

Opposite page: Lavender-blue flowers of 'Walker's Low' catmint (*Nepeta × faassenii* 'Walker's Low') and the upright purple flowers of the perennial 'May Night' salvia (*Salvia nemorosa* 'May Night') grab the eye in a curved flower border. Both are sun-loving perennials that are deer resistant and bloom in early summer. I chose them because their spike flowers combine well with the mounded, yellow-leaved deer-resistant shrub 'Goldmound' Japanese spirea. You can also insert some annuals to this scene. Try the low-growing, deer-resistant 'Purple Gnome' globe amaranth (*Gomphrena globosa* Gnome Purple) and the airy, white Diamond Frost® or Diamond Snow® euphorbia for color all summer.

68. THE SECRET GARDEN

Who hasn't dreamed of a secret garden? A walled-in sanctuary, cut off from the outside world, where flowers, fairies, and bees hold court. Such a garden that is separate from all else may not be possible for most of us, but we can create a secret garden, of a sort, by using a wall, a hedge, or a fence to form one side of a partially enclosed space. It does not have to be a large enclosure. In fact, the smaller it is, the more secret!

A rear corner of a backyard or an underused narrow side yard can become a secret garden if you define its boundaries in some way. Plant some shrubs to frame an opening or add a fence and gate to denote an entry portal. Make sure it is wide enough to accommodate a wheelbarrow. If a gate is not practical, an entry marker such as an overhead arbor, an upright stone, or a bird-bath can signify that this is a special place. I often locate a large planter filled with flowers to silently announce a transition from one area to another.

A sense of seclusion—a private world—is an important aspect of a secret garden. Overhead branches of a tree, a border of tall shrubs, or a tall wall can enhance that sheltered feeling. Within this cozy space, you may add plant beds bursting with greenery, some simple paving, a trickling recirculating fountain, or a small bench as the finishing touches.

And then there are the flowers—secret gardens must have flowers to beguile us. Imagine begonias spilling over in planters, dark-stemmed penstemon in plant beds, or corydalis growing out of an old stone wall. Frances Hodgson Burnett, in the classic 1911 book, *The Secret Garden*, describes the allure of such a hidden spot: "And the secret garden bloomed and bloomed and every morning revealed new miracles."

The ferny-leaved yellow corydalis (*Corydalis lutea*), a short-lived perennial, grows out of a stone wall in a secret garden. It sports pretty, yellow locket-shaped flowers that bloom from late spring through frost. Corydalis self-seeds prolifically and establishes itself in stone walls and gravelly soils in cool conditions. It practically thrives on neglect! It combines well with bleeding heart (*Lamprocapnos spectabilis*), lady's mantle (*Alchemilla mollis*), and other hardy perennials in a partial shade garden.

An entry of some kind says that a "secret garden" awaits you. This rustic portal is framed by an overhead cross beam, perfect for twining vines such as honeysuckle. Here, the vigorous climbing hydrangea grows over the fence to the right of the gate. Note the group of white-and-green 'Spring Green' tulips to the left of the entry. These are viridiflora tulips, named after the Latin for green (*viridi*). Each petal has a green streak in the center, finishing to an ivory white at the tips. This late-spring blooming tulip holds an RHS Garden of Merit award. This photo was taken at the outstanding public garden, Stonecrop Gardens, in Cold Spring, New York.

Any small area can be made into a secret garden. Here are the "before" and "after" photos of what became a small secret garden space for a dear client of mine. We added some rustic paving stones, low-growing plants, and lovely furniture to make it a sweet spot to sit and enjoy the garden. Now all it needs are some flowers . . .

69. BLUE AND YELLOW

Colors affect us on an emotional level. For example, deep blue appeals to many of us because it is so calming. If you combine it with a cheerful yellow, the results are even more satisfying. In fact, the blend of blue and yellow seems to be a favorite among gardeners and artists. Why? It may be that the steadfastness of blue blends well with the happiness of yellow. Such a color combination in a garden is sure to cheer anyone who visits it. I call it simply, Blue and Yellow.

Yellow flowers and foliage look their best—and glow the most—in the gentle rays of the morning or early evening sun. The sunlight at these times of day is on the red end of the light spectrum and enhances the warm colors: reds, oranges, and yellows. They shine in this kind of light.

Blue, on the other hand, is a cool, recessive or "shy" color. It needs the help of a stronger sun to be noticed. So blue blossoms stand out in the middle of the day when bright sun prevails. Together, the blend of blue and yellow ensures that a garden looks great at all times of day.

Blue and yellow flowers do well against a backdrop of shrubs such as holly, yews, Manhattan euonymus, or leatherleaf viburnums, among others. The dense green foliage is a perfect background for yellow's cheerful countenance and blue's soothing calmness. In addition, you can add a few pink flowers to the mix—they seem to bring out the blue flowers a bit more. A tip: plant both annual and perennial flowers to ensure that some flowers return each year. You can add long-blooming annuals in the spring.

Top: A group of tall annual sunflowers (*Helianthus annuus*) stands proud against a clear blue sky at the end of summer. This is a very simple way to have the joyous combination of yellow contrasted with blue in a garden. By the way, blue mixed with yellow makes green. So green fits in with this color scheme perfectly!

Bottom, left: The deep-blue flowers of the annual 'Victoria Blue' blue salvia (*Salvia farinacea* 'Victoria Blue') combine beautifully with the vibrant, yellow blooms of the 'Golden Butterfly' Marguerite daisy (*Argyranthemum frutescens* 'Golden Butterfly'). The latter is a tender perennial that is grown as an annual in cooler climates. It loves sun and is a cool season favorite. Its open, daisy-like flowers attract butterflies. The 'Golden Butterfly' is a newer cultivar and tolerates heat—cool night temperatures are best. It provides a burst of color all summer long. You can pair it with blue pansies and flowering kale in a Blue and Yellow Garden in the fall. Perennial in zones 10–11.

Bottom, right: A Blue and Yellow Garden need not be confined to flower colors. Here, a picket gate painted a deep blue makes a mysterious backdrop to the glowing yellow Darwin hybrid tulip, 'Blushing Apeldoorn.' I planted this variety of tulip for their extra-large flowers and bold blend of yellow, gold, and orange. They harmonize beautifully with the blue gate. Tulips bulbs need a cold period to establish roots, so they must be planted in the fall for spring flowers. Make sure to plant the tulip bulbs deep. This stops the plant from toppling over if you get a wet spring. It also allows you some room to plant atop them once their foliage has disappeared in early summer.

Top, left and right: Here are "before" and "after" photos of a woodland garden. We cleared out a 5-foot-wide path and edged it with small rocks, as seen on the left. We then planted the perennial white 'Deutschland' astilbe (*Astilbe japonica* 'Deutschland') in a large group behind the rock border. Deer and rabbit resistant, this hardy astilbe blooms in profusion in early summer, which is earlier than other white astilbes. It is a tried-and-true perennial for woodland gardens, tolerating semi-shade and shade conditions. Its brilliant white plumes stand out in a moonlight garden as well. Note the light pink blossoms of 'Peach Blossom' astilbe (*Astilbe japonica* 'Peach Blossom') that are mixed in. Zones 4–9.

Left: In spring, drifts of the native Virginia bluebells (*Mertensia virginica*) light up the woodland floor in the Steinhardt Garden in Mount Kisco, New York. Pink buds turn to varying shades of bright blue as they mature in April–May. This is a wonderful spring perennial plant for a woodland garden. Virginia bluebells grow 18 inches tall and prefer sun in early spring, followed by shade later as the trees leaf out. It seeds itself in the woods, forming large drifts. It goes dormant by midsummer and will disappear, so plant it with summer-blooming shade perennials like bugbane (*Actaea simplex*) and ferns to fill in once the bluebells fade. You can visit this garden through the Open Days program hosted by The Garden Conservancy. Zones 3–8.

70. HUNDRED ACRE WOOD

A woodland garden has a bit of magic about it, somewhat like Winnie-the-Pooh's fictional land, Hundred Acre Wood. This is where Pooh, Piglet, Tigger, and others from the Winnie-the-Pooh series of children's stories by British author A. A. Milne, lived. The Wood, which has captured the imagination of many Pooh fans, was based on Ashdown Forest in East Sussex, England. The Wood makes an enchanting theme for a woodland garden. Pooh, by the way, also offered great garden advice. I always liked his admonition that, "Weeds are flowers, too, once you get to know them."

Woodland gardens that are full of flowers are a collaboration between you and a certain Ms. Nature. A partnership with her in a forest setting is an unequal one, as you are imposing yourself on what is inarguably a perfect system. So if you intrude on Nature's domain, you must be mindful of the natural environment and follow her dictates. Once you do, the satisfaction of a sylvan garden retreat, awash in flowers, awaits you!

The most important consideration is that you do not disturb the all-important root systems of existing trees. Work respectfully around them and follow their lead for laying out paths and placing rocks and some soil. You may choose to create a wide mulched path, edged with small rocks, that winds through the woods. You can add shade-loving flowers along its edge. At the same time, it is a good idea to cut down any hazardous, dead, or sickly trees. Once an area is cleared, you can create open glades where ferns and flowers can brighten up the surroundings. Leave the tree trunks on the ground for nesting places for small animals. A downed tree also makes a rustic sitting bench, as Winnie-the-Pooh had in his Hundred Acre Wood.

The choice of flowers you plant depends on your particular site conditions. Native and shade-tolerant flowers such as great white trillium, mayapple, bleeding heart, columbines, and native coralbells work well in a wooded site in cool hardiness zones, because that is their natural habitat. Look at a plant's soil, sun/shade preference, and hardiness when choosing what to grow. Determine if you have dry shade and look for flowering plants that are suitable for that condition. Good choices include pulmonaria, vinca, lily of the valley, epimedium, and big root geranium.

71. OPEN HOUSE FOR BUTTERFLIES

Open House for Butterflies is a classic children's book by Ruth Krauss. Illustrated by Maurice Sendak, it shows a boy and a girl welcoming butterflies into their home and declares that an "open house for butterflies is a good thing to have." Just as fun, and much more practical, is a butterfly garden. This is probably the most enticing garden theme of all the ones I suggest. Who can say "no" to a butterfly garden?

Butterflies are mesmerizing as they fly through the landscape and pollinate flowers. They, along with dragonflies and bees, are treasured insects in many cultures. Butterflies seem almost magical as they flutter about. That may be one of the reasons why school butterfly gardens have exploded in popularity over the past decade. Kids love butterflies.

A more significant reason why butterfly gardens are being established in great numbers is that we are losing our butterflies due to habitat loss and pesticides. And we need them to pollinate flowers! So open house for butterflies is a very important thing to have. Here are a few tips to attract these marvelous creatures to your flowers. First, since butterflies are cold-blooded, they come to life as temperatures rise to around 85 degrees. So choose a sunny and warm location for your flower garden. Place a few large flat rocks among the flowers to give the butterflies a place to bask and warm up in the sun. If possible, locate the butterfly garden in a spot visible from your house so you can enjoy it as you look out.

Another helpful tip is to group flowers together in a single variety or color, as butterflies seem to find these groupings first. Butterflies are drawn to bright, vivid colors, including red, yellow, pink, orange, and purple. They love coneflowers, anise hyssop, bee balm, asters, cosmos, zinnias, sedum, and lantana, among others. Deadhead spent flowers often in order to ensure fresh nectar-laden blooms. Lastly, don't overclean your butterfly garden in autumn. Many beneficial insects and butterflies overwinter in plant debris and log and leaf piles. No leaf blowers here!

You can find some great books and websites that describe how to create a butterfly garden. For detailed information on how to create a certified butterfly garden, go to the website of the North American Butterfly Association (www.naba.org).

An eastern tiger swallowtail is large with bright yellow and black stripes. It is native to the eastern United States. Here, a tiger swallowtail feeds on a pink zinnia flower, one of its favorites. Zinnias and their nectar are also preferred by painted lady and monarch butterflies. These flowers are an important late-season nectar source for North American monarchs on their migration journey south to Mexico. Zinnias are one of the easiest annual flowers to grow from seed, and planting them is an excellent way to get children involved in butterfly gardening.

BUTTERFLY PUDDLING AREA

Butterflies will extract vital minerals and water from damp sand or soil in the garden.

Top, left: If you have limited space and want a hardy perennial flower that attracts butterflies, such as this monarch butterfly, plant a group of purple coneflowers (*Echinacea purpurea*). They bear large, daisy-like flowers of lavender-pink. Grows 30 to 36 inches high and blooms from mid-July through frost. Highly drought tolerant. It grows in light shade to full sun in a variety of soil types. Zones 3–8.

Top, right: Butterflies congregate around damp edges of puddles, or where water has evaporated and the ground is still moist. You can attract more butterflies to your garden by re-creating a shallow puddling pool. Fill a shallow dish such as a terracotta plant saucer or pie tin with gravel or pebbles. Bury it to the rim in a sunny, open spot where butterflies can land. Cover with a thin layer of water, leaving the tops of the rocks uncovered so the butterflies can perch on them as they sip. Butterflies crave the minerals and salts left behind as the water evaporates. Refill when needed. Add a small pinch of salt to the water to attract the butterflies. They typically visit puddling sites in the heat of a summer day.

A brilliantly colored monarch butterfly enjoys feeding on the vivid red-orange 'Torch' Mexican sunflower (*Tithonia rotundifolia* 'Torch'). This annual flower is an excellent butterfly flower and is easy to grow from seed. It features 2- to 3-inch open flowers that bloom prolifically from midsummer through fall. Grows to 5 feet tall and more on strong stems.

Top, left: Autumn fern (*Dryopteris erythrosora*) is a real stunner!
Although its name indicates a turn of color in the fall, it is the new
growth in spring of this evergreen fern that has an autumnal pinkish-
copper hue. The fronds then mature to a glossy green in summer.
Autumn fern grows to 24 inches tall and will flourish in high, open
shade and evenly moist soil. Zones 6–9. Here, I planted autumn fern
with the long-blooming and prolific blue-flowered geranium 'Rozanne.'
This perennial geranium grows in part shade and flowers through the
heat of midsummer. Zones 5–8.

Top, right: Japanese painted fern (*Athyrium niponicum* var. *pictum*) is
favored by gardeners for its luminescent gray-silver to white fronds.
Some varieties also have rich burgundy stems and midribs. The long,
triangular fronds tend to arch down to show off its tricolor markings,
perfect for edging a shady border. It was named 2004 Perennial Plant
of the Year by the Perennial Plant Association (PPA). Here, in part sun,
it adds a silvery accent to the annual vinca 'Pacifica XP Magenta Halo'
(*Catharanthus roseus* 'Pacifica XP Magenta Halo').

Left: The attractive short-lived perennial Arkwright's Campion
'Scarlet O'Hara' (*Lychnis × arkwrightii* 'Scarlet O'Hara') has gorgeous
orange-red blooms with five deeply notched petals. The showy flowers
are held above the foliage, and hummingbirds love them! It grows
18 inches tall, likes sun, and blooms from early to midsummer. Deer
resistant and self-seeds. Hardy in zones 3–9. Arkwright's Campion
makes a striking contrast to the upright and finely dissected fronds of
the native ostrich fern (*Matteuccia struthiopteris*). It, too, is deer resistant
and is at its full size of 3 to 6 feet in mid–late summer, after the campion
flowers have passed. A great combination. Hardy in zones 3–7.

72. FERNY GARDEN BOWER

What is a bower? This old-fashioned word has not been in use much, but I think it should come back. *Bower* means "a pleasant shady place under trees or climbing plants in a garden or wood." So if you have a half-shady spot beneath some trees or an arbor, no matter how small, you can refer to it as your bower. If the shade is too dense, consider removing a few lower tree branches to allow more sunlight in. It is here, in an area of dappled light, where ferns and shade-tolerant flowers can grow together.

Ferns are a wonderful choice for a bower garden. They naturally grow in warm, shady environments, are deer resistant, and their luxuriant foliage comes back every year after the plant goes dormant in the winter. Interestingly, ferns are an ancient plant group that dominated the landscape during the age of the dinosaurs. They were here before flowers appeared, and they reproduce asexually by means of spores that mature ferns release.

Ferns have no flowers, but their finely divided fronds (this is the term for fern leaves) are the show. The appearance of the fronds vary with the type of fern you plant. For example, Japanese holly fern (*Cyrtomium falcatum* Rochfordianum) has stiff, glossy, dark green fronds; while 'Burgundy Lace' Japanese painted fern (*Athyrium niponicum* 'Burgundy Lace') has silvery fronds tinged with burgundy-purple overtones. Various ferns planted together can make quite a display. Just make sure the ferns you choose match your hardiness zone.

Shade-tolerant flowers planted alongside ferns are a favorite combination of mine. Annual flowers are like long-lasting eye candy in a ferny bower garden. They keep flowering into fall when the ferns start to fade. Perennial flowers come back every year along with the fern fronds. It can be quite exciting when the fern fiddleheads and perennials poke their heads out of the earth in spring. Try a mix-and-match approach with ferns and flowers—if something looks out of place, feel free to dig it up and plant it elsewhere. It is important that the flowers have similar water and light requirements as the ferns.

73. KEEP CALM AND PURPLE–LIME GREEN

The "Keep Calm and Carry On" phrase has been modified many times, and I would like to add a new one: "Keep Calm and Purple–Lime Green." This saying may strike a chord in any gardener who likes this color combination. Purple blends the calm stability of blue with the hot energy of red. It uplifts the spirit and encourages creativity. Lime green, on the other hand, is associated with freshness and new growth. These two colors together, purple and lime green, make a dynamic duo, signifying creativity and renewal. No wonder this color combination is so popular in the garden.

You can have purple flowers in each season. In spring, tulips and alliums add a purple accent. Purple perennials for summer include false indigo, iris, agapanthus, lavender, catmint, and geranium 'Rozanne.' An unusual North American native perennial that blooms in summer is blue vervain (*Verbena hastata*). It has narrow candelabras of spikey panicles of small purple flowers. It creates a unique long-lasting vertical element in the garden. Blue vervain thrives in full or part sun in moist or wet soils, and it is suitable for USDA hardiness zones 3–9. The plants grow up to 2 to 6 feet tall. For late summer purples, look to blazing star, salvia, dahlia, asters, and phlox.

Lime green, or chartreuse, accent plants can include the lime-green cultivars of sweet potato vine (*Ipomoea batatas* spp.), golden Japanese forest grass (*Hakonechloa macra* 'Aureola'), Lemon Coral sedum (*Sedum mexicanum*), the lime-colored foliage of several coral bells varieties (*Heuchera* spp.), and more.

You can take the power of purple to the max in the landscape by pairing it with yellow, which is its complementary color. But the opposing contrast of these two colors vibrates with so much energy that it may be overwhelming. That is why lime green, which is a yellow-toned green, is a better match for purple flowers and purple foliage. Because lime green is not quite the opposite of purple, it makes a dramatic, yet not abrasive, pairing in the garden.

Lime-green flowers and foliage work well with both warm and cool color tones. This is helpful with the many shades of purple flowers. Cool-toned blue-purple flowers are seen as subdued and sophisticated. Their staid presence anchors a flower border. Red-purple or violet flowers are warm and vibrant. They seem to soften other colors. Lime green balances both the red and blue shades of purple and inserts an exhilarating "pop" to a landscape scene.

Above: Here, the annual flowers of deep-purple summer snapdragon (*Angelonia angustifolia*) and 'Titan Lilac' annual vinca (*Catharanthus roseus* 'Titan Lilac') contrast with the thin blades of the golden Japanese forest grass (*Hakonechloa macra* 'Aureola') and the large, lime-green leaves of sweet potato vine in the rear. Blue needleleaf evergreens add to the colorful display.

Right: In this watery scene, the luxuriant lobed foliage of 'Sweet Caroline Light Green' sweet potato vine (*Ipomoea batatas* 'Sweet Caroline Light Green') spills over the edges of a large metal plant container. The leaves remain light green throughout the season and the plant has excellent heat tolerance. It is balanced by the purple orchid-colored flowers of the annual New Guinea impatiens. This combination works well in planters and pots for a purple-lime green theme. This was at the annual Epcot International Flower & Garden Festival at Walt Disney World in Orlando, Florida.

Opposite page: The round pale purple flowers of edible chives (*Allium schoenoprasum*) appear in spring and summer on dark green stems rising above the foliage to 18 inches tall. Commonly used as a culinary herb to add mild onion flavor in cooking, these perennial plants also look lovely when paired with the herb golden oregano (*Origanum vulgare* 'Aureum'). Both are easily grown in average well-drained soils in full sun.

74. FOR THE BIRDS

If images of bright yellow goldfinches, black-capped chickadees, and vivid red cardinals in your backyard excite you, then a Garden for the Birds may be the theme for you. Besides being fun to watch, birds can be a powerful garden ally, because they eat harmful bugs such as cabbage worms, whiteflies, aphids, and grubs. Your flower garden can serve as a vital feeding station and sanctuary for our winged friends. And you will have the helpfulness of hungry, flitting birds to combat pests! The key is to provide food, water, and shelter for the birds. If you do that, you can enjoy a symphony of birdsong in your backyard. What a lovely and useful theme garden.

A surefire way to attract birds is to have a diverse mix of native flowers and berries for birds to enjoy. The more variety you offer, the better. While berried trees and bushes are a bird's delight, the right flowers attract them also. Birds like bright red, yellow, orange, and white. Native flowers such as Queen Anne's lace, black-eyed Susan, native asters, goldenrods, and yarrows provide seeds, nectar, and/or insects for birds to feed on. Other seed-bearing flowers that birds like include cosmos, sunflowers, zinnias, daisies, coreopsis, and marigold. These attract finches, sparrows, cardinals, nuthatches, and towhees in the fall. Another tip: avoid cutting down dead flower stalks with seeds attached, because seed-eating visitors like the dark-eyed junco, will benefit.

One of the most important elements to include in your bird habitat is water. Birds, like humans, need fresh, clean water to drink and bathe in. A properly sited birdbath, with a mister or dripper added, will attract a greater variety of birds than a feeder! Place a 3-foot-high bath in an open, sunny area that is somewhat sheltered. Here, birds can feel safe from lurking predators such as cats. Fill the bath with one or two inches of water and no more, because birds will not go into deeper water. Make sure the interior of the birdbath is consistently clean with no slippery surfaces—this is important. Clean it out often. A small birdbath dripper adds movement and sound to the water, which will get the birds' attention. Soon the birds will be splashing away.

Top, left: A fall scene features a rustic birdhouse set within a planting of the tall native perennial joe-pye weed (*Eutrochium purpureum*). Insectivorous birds love its flowers because they attract a multitude of insects to feast on. In the fall, joe-pye weed sets copious seeds that are eaten by such birds as goldfinch, Carolina wren, dark-eyed junco, and tufted titmouse. The plants are fairly resistant to browsing deer and rabbits. It grows from 4 to 7 feet in height, although there are shorter cultivars available. Its pale pink-purple flowers last from midsummer through early fall. This is in the New York Botanical Garden. Zones 4–9.

Top, right: The seed-bearing perennial 'Veitch's Blue' globe thistle (*Echinops ritro* 'Veitch's Blue') is an attractive addition to a bird-friendly garden. Its steel-blue, spherical flowers appear in early summer to midsummer, adding a unique color and texture. Globe thistle attracts pollinators and small birds, such as finches, that pick the smooth brown thistle seeds off the flowers. With globe thistle and sunflowers growing together in a sunny spot, you can offer birds a real treat! Drought tolerant and deer resistant. Zones 3–8.

Bottom: A classic birdbath is surrounded by Spanish bluebells (*Hyacinthoides hispanica*) in the late spring. Also known as the wood hyacinth, this perennial flower grows from a bulb planted in fall and multiplies over the years. The rigid flower stems arise from clumps of strappy foliage to show off bell-shaped, bluish-lavender blooms that open from the bottom up. This deer- and rodent-resistant perennial is an early season magnet for the bees. Hardy in zones 3–9.

75. NAMING YOUR GARDEN

Naming your garden instills warm feelings and creates an image for visitors to connect with. As the American playwright Eve Ensler notes, "I believe in the power and mystery of naming things. . . . I believe in naming what's right in front of us because that is often what is most invisible."

A garden that has a name is the first step toward making it "visible." For example, a flower patch can be named, Mom's Garden, and then, in a wink of an eye, the multicolored assortment of flowers that she plants every year outside the back door becomes a special place. This is true for other things as well—if you name your idea for a screenplay, then it is on its way to reality, and you now have to write it. Likewise, if you name your budding business, then it makes it easier to create those business cards and logo.

So go ahead and name that sunny spot in your yard, maybe Sunset Corner. Now you can create an intimate garden bathed in the blooms of late day and evening. Try planting the native wild-flower evening primrose (*Oenothera* spp.), which blooms at dusk, or try tropical four o'clocks (*Mirabilis jalapa*) and moonflowers (*Ipomoea alba*), which are nocturnal bloomers. If you name that low, always wet area Rain Garden, then a new world of floral possibilities opens up! Fill it with Japanese water iris (*Iris ensata*), golden ragwort (*Packera aurea*), turtlehead (*Chelone* spp.), and more. The name may come before the garden ever appears.

Placemaking depends on a name. This is true for a flower garden, as well. Brainstorm about names. It's fun, makes your garden "visible," and

gets the creative juices flowing. You can call an area the Lookout Garden or the Blue Border. Of course, I am assuming that the name you choose will be descriptive, but that may not be your style. I guess you could always name your garden Bob . . .

A special sign, fashioned from metal in the shape of a rising sun, happily announces an organic garden. It is a top part of an entry gate. The sun shines through the cut-out letters, lighting up the name.

Top: You can always call your garden, "Garden." 'Nuf said.

Bottom: Simple hand-painted signs can be made using a sanded board. Apply exterior house paint or craft paint to cover the entire board. Hand-letter the name using a paint pen. Once dry, you may choose to sand the board slightly to remove a little paint. It is a great way to make it look distressed and aged. Final touch: apply clear polyurethane over the sign to protect it.

The 20th-century English novelist and garden designer Vita Sackville-West said it best about cottage gardens: "It's cram, cram, cram, every chink and cranny." Do not be afraid to mix colors and crowd them in. I planted blue annual salvia 'Victoria Blue' throughout this bed and added all sorts of flower colors around it.

76. A FLOWERFUL COTTAGE GARDEN

Throw formality out the window and plant up a cottage garden! This kind of relaxed flower garden is known for a riot of colorful flowers jam-packed together with, perhaps, a winding path and picket fence to contain it. Imagine plant beds stuffed with coneflowers, hollyhocks, delphiniums, peonies, and even some vegetables—that is a cottage garden. The call of such an abundant scene, filled with fragrance from purple heliotrope and twining honeysuckle, makes one dizzy with anticipation. No wonder this garden theme is so popular.

In England, where cottage gardens originated, it seems everyone has such a garden, each more charming than the next. Their lushness sets a standard of perfection that is hard to achieve. But it is possible. What you need, at least in my part of the world, is a deer fence, deep fertile soil, constant watering, and someone to tend to it lovingly . . . a tall order indeed.

The backbone of a cottage garden are sturdy, reliable perennial flowers. In a sunny well-prepared plant bed (be sure to add that compost), set out a group of tall perennials in the rear of the bed and medium-tall ones in the mid-zone. You might try wild indigo (*Baptisia australis*), New England aster (*Symphyotrichum novae-angliae*), Siberian iris (*Iris sibirica*), dwarf gayfeather (*Liatris spicata* 'Kobold'), coneflowers (*Echinacea purpurea*), and Russian sage (*Perovskia atriplicifolia* 'Blue Spire'). Then add shorter flowers in front, making sure to include long-blooming annual flowers. Historically, cottage plantings were a blend of vegetables and flowers. So feel free to add some vegetables as well.

A low picket fence adds to the charm of a cottage garden. It also helps to keep out critters and supports tall flowers like garden phlox, Japanese wind anemones, and zinnias. The fence need not be a picket style. You may choose to install a bent willow, wrought iron, or lattice fence. The only suggestion is that the fence not be more than 42 inches high, because cottage gardens should project a friendly and inviting appearance. That is, after all, the true appeal of a cottage garden. It says, "Welcome to my garden; enjoy the flowers!"

The annual flower dianthus 'Telstar Picotee' F1 (*Dianthus chinensis × barbatus* 'Telstar Picotee' F1) makes a great edging plant in a cottage garden. Its fringed dark pink flowers bloom continuously all summer due to its excellent heat tolerance. I planted it here along a garden path that winds through the plantings. Go with a soft surface such as gravel or wood chips for an informal look.

77. THE WHITE GARDEN

Here's a tip that anyone can use in a flower garden: Plant white flowers. They make the whole garden sing. White blossoms glow in the evening, and their appearance cools us on hot days. White makes other colors stand out and injects serenity in any space. Who would think that simple white flowers would be so remarkable? If you look out on a gray day, you will see white-petaled blooms shining more than any other color amidst the green foliage. And you can plant white flowers anywhere in the landscape—as the French fashion designer Christian Dior said, "White is pure and simple and matches with everything."

The color white is elegant in any situation, and this is also true for white flowers. The statuesque white regal lily (*Lilium regale*), white rose, and white dahlia each add a stylish presence to any outdoor scene, especially when contained by clipped green boxwood or yew hedges. This is what the English gardener and author Vita Sackville-West did in her famous White Garden at Sissinghurst Castle in Kent, England. It is separated into individual areas by long rows of dark evergreen hedges and only white, green, gray, and silver plants grow within. These include white gladioli, white irises, white pompon dahlias, and white Japanese anemones, among others. The effect is magical!

You, like many gardeners, may be enthralled with the idea of a white garden. But before you plant, remember many white flowers are not pure white. Some have a yellowish or greenish cast, which makes it tricky to blend white flowers together. To help in this, interplant with green and white foliage plants such as Manhattan euonymus, 'Color Guard' yucca, or variegated Swedish ivy (*Plectranthus coleoides*). And plant silver plants to accentuate the white flowers. Try varieties of the silver-leaved artemisia such as 'Powis Castle,' the sculptural 'Miss Willmott's Ghost' (*Eryngium giganteum* 'Miss Willmott's Ghost'), and others.

Some white flowers can be playful and casual. Think of white Shasta daisies, airy white cosmos, white bleeding heart, baby's breath, and white pansies. All of these opalescent beauties are at home in a cottage-style white garden. Or try the annual deer-resistant white summer snapdragon (*Angelonia angustifolia*) for summer blooms, or the native perennial white wood aster (*Eurybia divaricata*) with its airy clouds of small white flowers for the fall. You can never go wrong with white flowers.

Top: A large clump of the graceful 'White Swirl' Siberian iris (*Iris sibirica* 'White Swirl') is stunning against a backdrop of still water. In late spring to early summer, the lavish display of rounded ruffled flowers features ivory-white falls that lead to a golden flush at the base. 'White Swirl' is considered one of the finest white Siberian irises. They require little care and have thick roots that like damp soil. They go down deep into the earth and are great for holding steep banks in place. After bloom, the slender, grassy leaves stand erect through the growing season. Deer resistant. Grows 30 to 36 inches tall. Zones 3–9.

Bottom, left: The graceful spires of white foxglove (*Digitalis purpurea alba*), with their pendulous bell-shaped flowers, are tall and perfect for the back of a bed. Plant them with white peonies, white 'Mount Everest' allium, and white garden phlox for a season-long white garden. Blooms late spring to summer. Self-sows. The leaves and seeds of this plant are highly toxic if ingested. Zones 4–8.

Bottom, right: The 'David' garden phlox (*Phlox paniculata* 'David') was named the 2002 Perennial Plant of the Year by the PPA for good reason. It is a midsummer bloomer that has dense heads of large, crisp-white, fragrant flowers. The round blooms are notably mildew resistant and bloom into early fall, which make it a winner! The snowy flowers can reach 3 feet high. Makes a great accent in a garden border in the summer. Zones 3–8.

Top, left: Striped water iris (*Iris laevigata* 'Variegata') is a vigorous perennial that is able to grow in 2 to 8 inches of standing water. Its wide cream-and-white striped leaves and stunning blue blooms, which appear in late May–early June, are outstanding. Grows 18 to 30 inches tall. Plant in large groups along ponds, streams, or in a damp location for a powerful effect. Great for rain gardens. The evergreen foliage retains its vertical striping all year. Sun to part shade. It likes moist, acidic soils. Deer resistant. Zones 4–9.

Top, right: Leichtlin's camass (*Camassia leichtlinii* Caerulea) likes moist, humusy, well-drained soils in sunny to part shady spots. It prefers soil that has a bit more moisture. It is a Pacific Northwest native that blooms in late spring and grows from a bulb. It has strappy leaves and beautiful star-shaped blue flowers that open from bottom to top on bare stems. Grows 24 to 30 inches tall. Naturalizes well. Zones 4–8.

Bottom, left: Striped water iris (*Iris laevigata* 'Variegata') at Coastal Maine Botanical Gardens shares the spotlight with well-placed rounded rocks. It thrives in standing water.

Bottom, right: Indian pink (*Spigelia marilandica*) is a native perennial wildflower that grows in moist woods and along shaded stream banks in the southeastern United States. It is eye-catching with bright red tubular flowers that narrow near the top and then flare out to show off five bright yellow tips. Indian pink flowers during May and early June, and it reaches 18 to 24 inches in height. It grows in medium-wet, well-drained soil in part shade to full shade. A favorite of butterflies and hummingbirds, its home turf is a bright woodland. Zones 6–9.

78. WET AND WILD

Do you have a low, soggy area in your lawn? A spot that is a giant puddle after a rain? Take this liability and make it your greatest asset—create a "rain garden" here, replete with moisture-loving flowers. I call this theme, Wet and Wild. Rain gardens are shallow, bowl-shaped depressions filled with plants. They are normally at the base of a hill or anywhere where water collects. These gardens accomplish their task by soaking up as much as 30 percent more water than conventional lawns, and they filter out pollutants from rainwater runoff. The flowers planted in these soggy sites also create a natural habitat for birds, butterflies, and other helpful insects.

To create a rain garden, start by digging out a basin in a naturally low, wet spot. It can be any size you want, but it must be at least 4 to 8 inches deep. Mound the excavated soil and stones on the downhill side of the depression to act as a dam of sorts. This prevents water from overflowing. The low mound is actually a plant bed, and so it should be wide and not too steep. Do not seed any lawn here. If your soil is heavy and does not drain, mix in some compost to lighten it up. It is important for the soil to contain organic matter, because a rain garden is like a living sponge of soil, fungi, and roots.

Plant the lowest, wettest part of the basin with perennials and shrubs that tolerate "wet feet" such as blue flag iris (*Iris versicolor*), Little Rocket ligularia, white turtlehead (*Chelone glabra*), or swamp milkweed (*Asclepias incarnata*). Around this, on upper areas, use plants that like regular moisture, such as New England aster (*Symphyotrichum novae-angliae*), blue false indigo (*Baptisia australis*), and boltonia (*Boltonia asteroides*). At the outside edge of the basin, place plants that prefer drier soil.

A few native perennial flowers to use in moist situations include Culver's root (*Veronicastrum virginicum*), great blue lobelia (*Lobelia siphilitica*), and eastern blue-eyed grass (*Sisyrinchium atlanticum*). Consider adding sedges, rushes, and ferns for diversity but also to create a thick root system that a functioning rain garden needs. A great source for rain garden information is the Rain Garden Alliance (raingardenalliance.org).

Marsh marigold (*Caltha palustris*) is a moisture-loving native flower in the buttercup family. It grows along streams and in wet woods. It is a mounded perennial with clusters of bright yellow flowers that appear in mid–late spring. Marsh marigold is known for its glossy, rounded heart-shaped leaves. It grows in full sun to part shade, and grows 1 to 2 feet tall. Hardy in zones 3–7.

79. A MIDSUMMER NIGHT'S DREAM GARDEN

Is there any theme more romantic than a flower garden based on Shakespeare's *A Midsummer Night's Dream*? One of the most popular plays by the great English playwright, it references 24 plants and flowers. For flower gardeners who love literary allusion, there can be nothing sweeter than King Oberon's description of the rustic retreat of his fairy queen, Titania:

> I know a bank where the wild thyme blows,
> Where oxlips and the nodding violet grows,
> Quite over-canopied with luscious woodbine.

Perhaps you might like to re-create a fairy queen's garden abode, abloom with the specific flowers mentioned: thyme, violets, oxlips, and the "luscious woodbine." This sweet spot is where you may encounter Puck from the fairy realm, and so you will need a place to sit and be lulled, as he said, "in these flowers with dances and delight." If you follow a gardening practice of Shakespeare's time, you may choose to build a low, wide stone seat on which to rest. The area at its base can be planted with creeping thyme (*Thymus serpyllum*). Its foliage releases an aromatic, pungent scent when sat upon or walked on.

Then add Titania's "nodding violets" to the scene. Plant the common blue violet (*Viola sororia*), a native spring-blooming perennial only 4 to 6 inches high. Please note that it freely self-seeds and spreads easily. A lawn tufted with clumps of violets in May fits well in a wild fairy queen's bower, but you may not want it to spread elsewhere.

Oxlip (*Primula elatior*) is also mentioned by King Oberon, but since it is a rare European native species why not use a relative? I suggest the spring-flowering polyantha primrose (*Primula × polyantha*). And Titania's hideaway was "over-canopied" with woodbine. That is the common name for European honeysuckle (*Lonicera periclymenum*), which is a deciduous twining climber that grows 10 to 20 feet tall. You can train this fragrant flowering vine up a trellis near the stone seat to create a partial green enclosure. The tubular, two-lipped flowers appear from early to late summer and are highly scented at night. A midsummer night's dream, indeed.

Top: Creeping thyme (*Thymus serpyllum*) is a somewhat woody, very low-growing perennial. It forms a mat of foliage 2 to 3 inches tall, which spreads over time by rooting stems. When it is stepped on, it perfumes the air. You can plant it among stepping stones, as shown here. Also called mother-of-thyme, it is densely flowering, with deep pink to purple flowers that appear in summer on short stems. Bees love its tiny flowers, and the honey they make from thyme blossoms is aromatic. Creeping thyme has cultivars with dark green, lime-green, or variegated foliage. It grows in full sun and tolerates drought and dry, shallow soil. Zones 4–8.

Bottom, left: Low-growing common violets (*Viola sororia*), with their heart-shaped leaves, is a native found throughout eastern North America. It is very easy to grow as a ground cover under shrubs or larger perennials. In spring, it is covered with small purple flowers that serve as an early nectar source for pollinators. Violets thrive in cool, moist, shady conditions but also tolerate drought. It forms colonies and spreads by seed or short rhizomes. Try the cheerful cultivar 'Freckles' (*Viola sororia* 'Freckles') with its white flowers speckled with deep China blue. Flowers are edible! The leaves and stems of violets are rich in vitamins A and C. Zones 3–9.

Bottom, right: 'Scentsation' honeysuckle (*Lonicera periclymenum* 'Scentsation') is an extremely fragrant vining honeysuckle with showy yellow flowers that bloom from mid-spring to late summer. The flowers are followed by bright red berries. 'Scentsation' grows to 10 to 15 feet tall, and it is not invasive like other honeysuckles. Full sun. Zones 4–9.

80. FALL FLOWER DELIGHT

When fall arrives, the days become cool and the sun, being lower in the sky, throws a vivid spotlight on trees and their changing cloaks of color. Autumn's shorter days also trigger certain late-blooming perennials to open their flowers and delight us. They have quietly been growing through the summer and now, when other perennial flowers start to go dormant, chrysanthemums, anemones, asters, dahlias, and toad lily cheerfully celebrate the brilliance of fall. They are prime candidates for an end-of-the-growing-season flower garden. You can revel in the crisp air and clear blue skies, knowing that autumn is, as the 19th-century American poet William Cullen Bryant described, "the year's last loveliest smile."

A Fall Flower Delight garden is a sweet way to exult in the quiet moments of autumn. Find a sunny spot that you can view from a warm house and make a wide plant bed. Amend the soil amply with compost. Go beyond the standard autumn palette of deep red and bright yellow chrysanthemums and include lavender asters, pink dahlias, sedum 'Autumn Joy,' and vivid white Montauk daisies. In spring, plant annuals such as the apricot-hued 'Unbelievable Lucky Strike' begonia and the orange 'Luscious Marmalade' lantana among the nascent fall-blooming perennials. The warm-toned annuals will bloom all summer and will be ready for some companionship when the asters, dahlias, and others finally open up.

A striking fall flower, an annual in cooler climes, is the showy Mexican bush sage (*Salvia leucantha*) that blooms purple, white, or bicolor on tubular flower spikes that rise above the foliage. This bushy subshrub flowers from late summer to frost, grows 2 to 3 feet tall, and adds a vertical accent to any fall garden. It is best in full sun and is suitable for USDA hardiness zones 8–10. Plant this along with the thread-leaf bluestar (*Amsonia hubrichtii*), a three-season perennial performer that features clusters of sky-blue flowers in late spring and finely textured bright green foliage that turns a rich yellow in the fall. The thread-leaf bluestar was named the 2011 Perennial Plant of the Year by the Perennial Plant Association (PPA).

The soft pink, slightly cup-shaped flowers of Japanese windflower (*Anemone × hybrida* 'Robustissima') float in the breeze 3 to 4 feet above mounded foliage in late summer through October. This windflower is a star in a fall flower garden, blooming for weeks. A vigorous perennial, 'Robustissima' windflowers like evenly moist, well-drained soils in sun to part shade. Beware—they live up to their "robust" name and may naturalize in the garden by spreading rhizomes to form large colonies. They are easy to grow and are deer and rabbit resistant. May need extra winter mulch in colder areas. Zones 4–7.

Top, left: Chrysanthemums, or mums as they are often called, are a fall favorite because of their amazing range of colors and bloom types. They respond to shorter daylight hours for flowering and are at their zenith between August and October. They like moist, well-drained soil in full sun. Cut stems back with a pair of sharp pruners from late spring to midsummer (Memorial Day to July 4) to encourage compact, bushy growth. After they flower, cut these perennials back to 8 inches high and mulch in winter. Mums are somewhat resistant to deer and rabbits. Zones 5–9.

Top, right: 'Hillside Sheffield Pink' chrysanthemum (*Chrysanthemum rubellum* 'Hillside Sheffield Pink') is a vintage mainstay of the fall garden. It is a clump-forming perennial that starts out with medium pink buds in early fall that open into gorgeous single daisy-like apricot-pink flowers with yellow centers in October. It grows 24 inches tall and 36 inches wide, and it is a vigorous addition to any flower garden. 'Hillside Sheffield Pink' tolerates heat and drought, and it is perfect for a sunny rock garden, as shown here. Pinch back hard in early June to keep plants compact. Long, blooming flowers are attractive to butterflies. This is at the Steinhardt Garden in Mount Kisco, New York. You can visit this garden through the Open Days program of The Garden Conservancy (www.gardenconservancy.org/open-days). Zones 4–7.

Left: The native perennial bluestar (*Amsonia hubrichtii*) was discovered growing in the wild in the early 1940s. It is native to south-central United States. It is a great filler in the flower garden— easily grown in average, medium, well-drained soil in full sun to part shade. It has powdery blue star-like flowers in late spring. Its best fall foliage color occurs in full sun. Cut back stems by 6 inches after flowering to keep plants as a neat foliage mound. Zones 5–8.

Top, left: There are more than 4,000 bee species in the United States, but they are in peril due to our overuse of pesticides and herbicides. Bee-friendly gardens, with blue salvia as shown here, are a way we can help Nature restore balance. Plant flowers and native wildflowers that provide loads of nectar to help our endangered bees. Bees are able to smell and detect nectar with a high concentration of sugar, so they will find them. Bees can see white, yellow, blue, and even UV colors. Bees cannot see red.

Top, right: If there is one flower to plant in a bee garden, this is it! The silvery mountain mint (*Pycnanthemum muticum*) is a native perennial that is one of the best nectar sources for bees and native butterflies. It is a 3-foot-tall plant with densely packed, small tubular pink flowers with underlying showy, leaflike silver bracts. It naturalizes and spreads by rhizomes, so it may need to be divided after a few years. Mountain mint is loaded with pulegone, a clear, oily liquid that acts as a mosquito repellent when rubbed on the skin! Zones 4–8.

Left: Here, a bee forages on the tubular, lavender-blue flowers of 'Blue Fortune' anise hyssop (*Agastache* 'Blue Fortune'). Bees, butterflies, and hummingbirds love the bottlebrush-like flowers, which are filled with nectar. This licorice-scented perennial thrives in sun and dry soils, and they are perfect for an herb garden or mixed border. Grows 2 to 3 feet tall and is hardy in zones 4–9. According to The Honeybee Conservancy (www.thehoneybeeconservancy.org), bees are a wonderful way for children to learn about ecology, agriculture, and mutual cooperation.

81. A BEE-FRIENDLY GARDEN

Did you know that bees are responsible for roughly one in every three bites of food we eat? That is because they pollinate flowers which, in turn, form seeds, fruits, nuts, beans, and vegetables. Our food supply depends on bees and other pollinators—they are our literal lifeline. Yet we are destroying the bees with our use of harmful pesticides and the destruction of their habitat. Bees in the United States are dying at an unprecedented rate.

Pollination begins as bees forage for the sweet elixir called nectar that is held within a flower. Nectar gives bees energy. And the pollen they collect is like protein. As a bee goes inside a flower to drink the nectar, it picks up pollen grains that stick to the hairs of their bodies. It then carries those pollen grains from flower to flower, which initiates fruiting.

You can help the bees by planting a Bee Garden filled with nectar-rich flowers. By doing so, you will be making our world a healthier place for honeybees, mason bees, bumblebees, solitary bees, and others. A Bee Garden is pesticide-free and can be any size and be anywhere. A planter full of flowers is perfectly fine. Just be sure not to use any insecticides on your plants and, when purchasing flowering plants, look for a label that says they are neonic-free. That is short for neonicotinoids, a class of pesticide that concentrates in the pollen (and more). It contributes strongly to the killing of bees. Also, during the growing season, remove dead blooms to prolong the blooming period of certain flowers.

Bees are drawn to flat, open blooms with big petals for easy landings, or tubular flowers with lots of pollen and nectar. Plant a variety of flower shapes to accommodate bees with different tongue sizes. Single flowers such as daisies, pansies, black-eyed Susans, asters, helenium, and marigolds make nectar and pollen more accessible to bees than showy, double flowers. The frilly, hybridized ones produce less nectar so opt for the original flowers.

Bees prefer white, yellow, blue, and purple blooms. They do not perceive red. Honeybees remember which colored flowers are a good source of pollen. If they find a blue flower that is rich in pollen on a trip, they will visit more blue flowers on subsequent trips rather than hopping among different colors. This is unlike bumblebees and other native bees, which forage on diverse, native wildflowers. For more info on creating a pollinator-friendly garden in your region, go to the website of the Pollinator Partnership (www.pollinator.org/guides).

82. THE WILD GARDEN

If you'd like your landscape to look as if it were planted by Nature, then an informal Wild Garden is the theme for you. This naturalistic plant-driven approach to gardening was originally popularized by the 19th-century English gardener William Robinson, who turned away from the fussy Victorian flower gardens of his time and advocated, in his popular books, the use of plants that were in tune with the surrounding natural landscape. He suggested following Nature's dictates and mixing desired plantings with exotic plants. He also advocated for swaths of bulbs planted in grass. His ecological sensibility and advice heralded the transformation of flower gardens into the sustainable gardens we strive for in the 21st century.

In 1870, Robinson published his revolutionary book, *The Wild Garden*. He encouraged gardeners to adapt Nature's loose look and to respect plant form, color, and growing habits rather than imposing a rigid layout on the land. He followed that influential book with *The English Flower Garden* in 1883. In this book he promoted the study of the interaction of plants and how each one's size and foliage worked with others. These two books presaged a more respectful understanding of the natural world and its workings, and they introduced the world to a new approach to garden design.

The aim of a Wild Garden is to nurture local biodiversity with native and introduced plants. You must be mindful of your site and know its light, soil, and climate, because plants in wild gardens are specific to the ecology. Plants are grouped together based on common habitat, such as woodland, droughty, prairie, or wetland. Scale does not matter—you can have a wild garden of perennials and grasses in an open expanse or in a window box.

William Robinson's ideas on natural ecological design continue to resonate today. A newly designed edition of *The Wild Garden* has been created by expert and author Rick Darke. It illustrates the wild garden approach and explains why it is so relevant for today's gardeners, designers, and landscape professionals.

Top: The green-and-white blades of variegated Japanese iris (*Iris ensata* 'Variegata') are at home in the saturated soil near a rustic pond. Perfect for a moist wild garden, the vertical, striped leaves look good even without the lovely, drooping purple flowers that appear in early summer. Likes full sun or partial shade and grows 35 inches tall. Keep moist. Zones 4–9. You can see this at the Phillis Warden garden in Bedford Hills, New York, through the Open Days program of The Garden Conservancy.

Bottom, left: In this partially shady wet site, I elaborated on the wildflower garden theme by intermingling fluffy native ostrich ferns (zones 3–7) with the dark green-leaved perennial bugbane (*Actaea simplex*), seen in front. Bugbane grows 3 to 4 feet tall and is hardy in zones 3–8. Along with those plants, I added annuals (red angel wing begonias and blue salvia) for a pop of color.

Bottom, right: Informal stone and gravel steps are bordered by a wild-looking assortment of plants. This is in the dry Wild Garden at Wave Hill, a public garden in the Bronx, New York. The airy purple flowers of the tender perennial tall verbena (*Verbena bonariensis*) contrast with the wispy, wheat-colored Mexican feather grass (*Nassella tenuissima*). Both plants are hardy in zones 7–10 and both like heat and full sun. They are grown as annuals in cooler areas.

bok choi
Brassica rapa
(Chinensis Group) 'Red Choi'
BRASSICACEAE

83. CABBAGES AND KINGS

Let's talk cabbage! As the Walrus said in Lewis Carroll's famous poem, "The Walrus and the Carpenter":

> To talk of many things:
> Of shoes—and ships—and sealing-wax—
> Of cabbages—and kings—

I want to talk about ornamental cabbage and kale, the colorful leafy sentinels of fall gardens. Although they are foliage plants and in the same plant family as broccoli and Brussels sprouts, cabbage and kale rival flowers for their colorful beauty and form in the fall. The term *ornamental cabbage* refers to varieties with broad, unruffled leaves. The bottom half of their foliage remains green, while the rosettes in the center turn bright purple, pink, or white. The overall effect resembles a huge blossom. Ornamental kale is similar except that the leaves are wavy-edged, deeply ruffled, or curly. They provide a fall finale of color to any setting! Ornamental cabbage and kale are both grown as annuals and are very cold hardy.

Technically, ornamental cabbage and kale are both kales, since they do not form heads. And, although edible, ornamental cabbage and kale leaves are bitter and are best grown for the elegant foliage. They do not require a lot of care—no pinching, pruning, or staking. All they need is the cool weather of spring or fall to develop their best color. As night temperatures drop below 50 degrees, the leaf color darkens and intensifies. This is why ornamental cabbage and kale add such a vibrant punch to cool season flower beds and planters.

You can buy small plants of ornamental cabbage and kale. Simply place them where their colorful foliage can be admired, such as the front of a border or in planters. You can group them together for impact, but they are also quite impressive when used singly next to fall perennials, such as dark-leaved sedums (*Sedum* spp.) or annual love-lies-bleeding (*Amaranthus caudatus*) or chrysanthemums (*Chrysanthemum* spp.). Or you can plant one large, blossom-like ornamental cabbage or kale in a small flowerpot alone—it makes a happy sight by the front door.

Top, left: The frilly, deep purple-red leaves of 'Redbor' kale (*Brassica oleracea* 'Redbor') add intense color and texture in the fall flower garden. 'Redbor' kale, with its almost completely red coloring from rib to leaf tip, is an excellent replacement for waning summer annuals. Its purple color contrasts brilliantly with the orange and yellow colors of autumn. The magenta, blue, and silver of the kale are compelling accents. 'Redbor' is an upright plant, growing at least 2 feet tall on strong stems, with tightly curled foliage. Full sun to part shade. Pair with asters, dusty miller, mums, 'Profusion' zinnias (as shown), or pansies. Zones 2–11.

Top, right: Ornamental cabbage forms a tight rosette of magenta leaves in the center, creating a unique, cold-hardy "blossom" of sorts. Add these plants to a fall garden amidst pumpkins, grasses, and late-blooming flowers. The magenta color darkens in the cool days of fall. The most intense coloration occurs when night temperatures range between 35 and 45 degrees.

Bottom, left: 'Osaka Red' compact cabbage cultivar has an outer ring of semi-wavy purple leaves surrounding a vibrant magenta center. When planted together with other cabbage varieties in a rounded, ribbed planter such as this, the effect is stunning. Although they are not flowers, they certainly give that appearance in the cool days of fall.

Bottom, right: Beautiful dark red leaves of 'Red Choi' bok choi (*Brassica rapa* var. *chinensis* 'Red Choi') look great along with dark pink pansies. Bok choy is best eaten when its leaves are young and have a mild flavor. Sow seeds from early spring through mid-summer. In the southern United States, fall seeding is possible. Try the variety called 'Rosie' for its bright strawberry-red leaves.

84. A FRAGRANCE GARDEN

> "I have a notion that *smell*, not sight, is the most mystical sense.
> The garden has persuaded me of this."
> —VIGEN GUROIAN, *THE FRAGRANCE OF GOD*

Imagine sitting among your favorite shrubs and flowers, inhaling beautiful scents, hearing the birds sing, and feeling the warm air. The aroma wafts around you and tickles your nose. Time, for a second, stands still and your blood pressure drops and you relax. Why does breathing in flowers' fragrance affect us so markedly? The secret is that fragrance travels into our brain immediately.

Volatile compounds, the small organic molecules that make up strong fragrances, enter our bloodstream through the nose. They can cross the blood-brain barrier and have a direct effect in the brain by acting on receptor sites. This immediacy produces wonderful results. For example, the scent of lavender (*Lavandula* spp.) flowers has been found to help people increase alertness and accuracy when taking math tests. Similarly, the "cherry pie" fragrance of purple heliotrope flowers can envelope you in well-being, while citrus scents literally make us happy. Once we know this, it is hard not to plant a Fragrance Garden.

Many flowers produce a scent, the most famous being the rose and jasmine. But why not try other wonderful perennial and annual flowers that emit sweet smells? These include the easy-care, yellow Hyperion daylily (*Hemerocallis* × Hyperion), the shade-tolerant woodland phlox (*Phlox divaricata*), and the long-blooming bee balm (*Monarda didyma*), among others. Beware of genetically modified hybrid flowers—sometimes the scent is bred out of them in favor of size.

Fragrant gardens do best when the air is warm, because the scents carry better. Plant several fragrant flowers in a sunny, sheltered corner or against a wall. Partially enclosed spaces concentrate the plants' scents within the space. Plant tall, fragrant, flowering shrubs like lilac as a backdrop to your fragrant garden. And locate low-growing, sweet-scented perennials, annuals, and herbs along the front borders of your Fragrance Garden. If you plan well, you can have fragrance growing there from spring to fall.

Fragrance is memory's powerful keeper. A whiff of gardenia or heliotrope or other flowers can take us back to an earlier time in our life. Surround yourself with lavender, lemon verbena, and chamomile. Add a small table and chair for afternoon tea in the garden. How enchanting!

Top, left: All lilies are aromatic, but the Stargazer lily (*Lilium* Stargazer), a hybrid variety of the Oriental group, is the most fragrant of all. Its bowl-shaped blooms explode in pink to crimson, with white edges and dark spots. Its luscious petals stretch outward. But it is the slightly spicy scent that is so striking. When Stargazer lilies cast their aroma across the garden you can smell it throughout. I planted it here with dwarf black-eyed Susan (*Rudbeckia fulgida* var. *sullivanti* 'Goldsturm') and Russian sage (*Perovskia atriplicifolia*). It blooms in mid- to late summer. Zones 4–9. *Photo by Laura Hendrix McKillop.*

Top, right: The large, fragrant, double white blossoms of 'Aphrodite' hosta (*Hosta plantaginea* 'Aphrodite') appear above glossy foliage from late July to September. A cultivar of the aptly named August Lily, 'Aphrodite' is one of the most fragrant hostas available. Attractive to butterflies and hummingbirds. Zones 5–8.

Bottom, left: I like the honey-scented fragrance of the low-growing, mounding annual flower, sweet alyssum (*Lobularia maritima*). It is a perfect edging plant. The hybrid 'Snow Princess' alyssum is tolerant of hot summer temperatures and is covered with clusters of sweetly fragrant, tiny white flowers from spring to frost. It grows 2 to 3 feet across and 1 to 2 feet high.

85. TINY SPACE, TINY GARDEN

There is no space too small for a flower garden! If an outdoor area has soil, a source of water, and can hold small plants or potted plants, then it can be home to a little green world, blooming with color. It might be a narrow area behind the top of a low wall, or it might be a long planter box at the base of a balcony railing. I have made small gardens on strips next to sidewalks. Flowers are remarkably resilient, given some care and attention.

A tiny outdoor space lends itself to becoming a small-scale fantasy land, an enchanting habitat where fairies may reign. For a whimsical Fairy Garden, all you need are low-growing, resilient plants and imagination. In this miniature landscape, you can cover the ground with moss, creeping thyme, sedum, and Corsican mint. Annual celosia and lavender topiary can be used as trees. Small sedums work well, too. Rustic huts may be fashioned from natural materials such as driftwood. Seashells, broken pots, pine cones, and rounded stones add fun and interest.

It is fun to use small flowering plants as tiny landscape elements. A good example is sea thrift, a compact perennial that is tolerant of salt and is often applied on sidewalks and driveways in winter. It looks like a little grassy hill. The blue, furry flowers of the deer-resistant, low-growing annual floss flower (*Ageratum houstonianum*) can be used to emulate a blue hydrangea. Need a lawn? Add the fast-growing, blue star creeper (*Isotoma fluviatilis*) to form a carpet of tiny green leaves that are covered with starry, soft-blue flowers in the summer. It is ideal for planting between stones, and it is suitable for USDA hardiness zones 5–9. Or plant baby's tears (*Soleirolia soleirolii*) as a dense green ground cover.

Compact, little spaces may require you to keep some plants in their pots to help them retain their size and stay small. Simply plant the container directly in the soil. Water often, because plants in pots dry out more rapidly.

Top: A tiny fairy garden sits above a concrete retaining wall in a narrow space next to a parking lot. The driftwood hut is set within a slope that's held in place by grassy sea thrift (*Armeria maritima*). It has purplish-pink, ball-shaped flowers arising from tight mounds of evergreen foliage. These tough little perennial wonders grow 6 to 12 inches high and bloom from mid-spring through early summer. Zones 4–8. The red feathery flowers of the annual plumed cockscomb (*Celosia argentea* var. *plumosa*) make a colorful backdrop, and white alyssum adds a sweet touch.

Bottom, left: A small standing Buddha is part of a tiny shady garden. Moss covers the earth and a stone anchors the scene. White flowering annual vinca (*Catharanthus roseus*) look like small shrubby plants next to the diminutive figure. This is atop an outdoor retaining wall in a partially sunny corner.

Bottom, right: A small door, about 14 inches high, at the base of a tree is a whimsical addition to any fairy garden. This is at the Harry P. Leu Gardens in Orlando, Florida.

86. A BURLE MARX–INSPIRED MODERN FLOWER GARDEN

"Do not the prolific blossoms on a plant manifest happiness?
Sometimes I would like to think so."
—ROBERTO BURLE MARX

One of the foremost landscape architects of the 20th century was a Brazilian artist, Roberto Burle Marx, who loved plants and flowers. His colorful, exuberant landscapes were like modernist paintings transferred to the garden, and they were revolutionary for his time. His tremendous influence on landscape design continues today. These designs are known for free-form masses of color and the bold use of tender bedding plants to create painterly effects in the landscape. He was ahead of his time in that he advocated the preservation and use of native flora. However, he used common adaptable plants from all over the world as well as some that were rare.

Burle Marx treated landscape design as a living art, and he was passionate about the wonders of Nature. He once asked, "Why does nature, with the one hand, create a leaf so broad and tough that a child can float on, and with the other, fashion a flower as tiny as a pinhead containing all the organs for its reproduction?" His curiosity knew no bounds. He was a plant explorer as well as a horticulturist and designer. His gardens, mostly tropical, were a celebration of all plants.

You can incorporate the artful planting ideas of Burle Marx to create a bold and striking garden of your own. Follow his use of curvilinear shapes for flower beds. Plant a large rounded, free-form mass of flowers within an existing bed or in a bed all its own in an open lawn. Use a plant palette bursting with high-contrast colors. Try colorful red coleus and yellow marigolds or, in partial shade, plant large-leafed caladiums amidst a large grouping of New Guinea impatiens.

Burle Marx adapted his love of color and form to the garden in artful ways. We can follow his lead and make prolific flower gardens that are both playful and pollinator friendly. In so doing, we may, to use his wise words, "manifest happiness."

Left: The bold duo of vibrant orange bromeliads (*Aechmea blanchetiana*) set in a sea of bright pink summer snapdragons (*Angelonia angustifolia* 'Angelface Pink') was part the memorable 2019 exhibit dedicated to Roberto Burle Marx at the New York Botanical Garden. It reflects his love of high-contrast color and flowers.

Below: An expansive tropical garden was the highlight of the New York Botanical Garden exhibit, *Brazilian Modern: The Living Art of Roberto Burle Marx* in 2019. Raymond Jungles, his student and well-known landscape architect, designed this landscape using the plant palette and design ideas of his mentor.

"Everyone should have themselves
regularly overwhelmed by Nature."
—GEORGE HARRISON

A FEW CHOICE PERENNIAL FLOWERS TO TRY

Perennials—those flowering plants that seem to die every winter but come back the following spring—are reminders that Nature works in cycles. The seasonal rhythms of perennial flowers keep us mindful that the "flow" never stops. In spring, snowdrops, daffodils, irises, and peonies emerge from the ground to serenade us. They are followed by a procession of perennial flowers that feed our pollinators—and our spirits—through the summer into the late fall. It is a never-ending dance of floral color, fragrance, and form that Nature uses to attract insects and birds. For example, when coneflowers open each summer, it doesn't take long for the bees to find them. Soon after, the goldfinches appear to feast upon the mature seeds. And then, in winter, the coneflower plant dies down only to reappear and start again in the spring.

The reason perennials are so popular is that, for the most part, these returning flowers, especially those native to a region, do not require much care, watering, or feeding, once they are established. Their blooms appear at the same time each year, like clockwork, and continue flowering for weeks. To enjoy the show, you need to know a little about the perennial you are planting—which soil it likes, how much water it requires, and which sun and shade conditions it needs. A perennial flower that likes full sun needs at least seven to eight hours of direct light daily in order to thrive. If it does not get adequate sun, you'll get a lackluster plant and minimal blooms.

So how to know which perennial flowers to grow? This chapter, "A Few Choice Perennial Flowers to Try," discusses some of my personal flower favorites. It is not a comprehensive list by any means, but just a few that I have found to be especially reliable. I have selected sturdy bloomers that are relatively easy to care for and primarily suited for cooler hardiness zones. I note any that have been selected as a Perennial Plant of the Year by the Perennial Plant Association (PPA). These are outstanding perennials suitable for a wide range of growing climates, require low maintenance, have multiple-season interest, and are relatively pest- and disease-free.

Many new cultivars of our favorite perennial flowers are arriving on the market every year. I cannot include all of their names, but I urge you to look at the new flower introductions and get detailed planting instructions in catalogs, magazines, and on the Internet. Also ask your local garden center for their recommendations on the best varieties to grow in your area. Once you enjoy seeing these beauties return each year in your garden, I hope you will expand beyond this introductory list.

Above, left: The native daisy-like flower *Coreopsis*, commonly known as tickseed, is a low-maintenance, drought-tolerant, long-blooming perennial that is easy to grow. Their profuse blooms are delightful in early summer. Goldfinches love to snack on the seeds during fall and winter. There are many cultivars of coreopsis in colors from yellow and orange to pink and red. Sun and well-drained soil. Zones 4–9.

Top, left: 'Fatal Attraction' coneflower (*Echinacea purpurea* 'Fatal Attraction') are in full bloom, with summer-blooming ornamental onion (*Allium*) in the background. *Photo by Laura Hendrix McKillop.*

Top, center: 'Millenium' ornamental onion (*Allium* 'Millenium'), named 2018 Perennial Plant of the Year by the Perennial Plant Association (PPA). Deer resistant.

Top, right: Butterfly weed (*Asclepias tuberosa*), named 2017 Perennial Plant of the Year by the PPA. Generally deer resistant.

Left: Lenten rose (*Helleborus × hybridus*), named 2005 Perennial Plant of the Year by the PPA. Deer resistant.

Right: Bluestar (*Amsonia hubrichtii*), named 2011 Perennial Plant of the Year by the PPA. Deer resistant.

87. THE BEAUTIFUL GOLD VARIEGATED SWEET IRIS

If you need a tough, drought-tolerant flowering plant with deliciously scented lavender-blue flowers and showy tricolored foliage, look no further than the gold variegated sweet iris (*Iris pallida* 'Variegata Gold'). It is a deer-resistant perennial that has upright sword-shaped leaves with vertical bands in gray-green and creamy yellow. A real eye-catcher, even when not in bloom, it grows easily in well-drained soil with low to average fertility. It can grow in sun to part shade conditions. *Iris pallida* was found in Croatia and is resistant to borers. Divide it in late summer every third or fourth year to keep it blooming. Its bearded iris-type flowers appear in late spring to early summer atop scapes rising to 40 inches tall. The foliage is 32 to 36 inches tall. It is suitable for USDA hardiness zones 4–9.

The vertical blades of *Iris pallida* blend with other perennials nicely. Since irises grow from underground rhizomes, which look like tubers, they can be tucked easily around other plants. It's fun to place them with companion plants that bloom later to keep the floral display going. Look for annuals or perennials that contrast with the iris foliage or can fill in around it.

Some companion perennials for irises are those that bloom later in the summer and are around the same height or shorter. These include dwarf black-eyed Susan, 'Snowcap' Shasta daisy, perennial geraniums, sedum, and yarrow. Of course, you can pop in annuals such as spring pansies and summer blooming angelonia to make it one glorious scene!

Interestingly, the rhizomes of *Iris pallida* are used to produce orris root, which is used as a fixative in perfumes. It also provides a base note in the fragrance of Chanel No. 5 and others. Dried orris root has an earthy, sweet scent that resembles the fragrance of violets or raspberries. Orris oil is also added to some types of popular gin, including Bombay Sapphire.

Above: The upright, striped blades of sweet iris grow next to another blue-flowering. deer-resistant perennial: catmint (*Nepeta*). The catmint blooms just a little later than the sweet iris.

Opposite page: Gold variegated sweet iris (*Iris pallida* 'Variegata Gold') is luminous with its striped gold-and-green leaves. It is especially lovely when planted in front of a dark green backdrop such as a boxwood or holly hedge, as shown here. Sweet iris blends well with other perennials such as *Stachys* 'Hummelo,' candytuft, and perennial blue salvia. It is easy to grow and care for—a winner for any landscape. Deer resistant. Zones 4–9.

88. GERANIUM 'ROZANNE'— PLANT OF THE CENTENARY

In 2013, the Royal Horticultural Society (RHS) announced its Plant of the Centenary—the best plant introduced at the RHS Chelsea Flower Show in the United Kingdom in the last hundred years (1913–2013). They chose geranium 'Rozanne' as the best overall plant. If you see this plant in bloom, you will know why they chose it. 'Rozanne' geranium is a hardy perennial that requires little attention and is covered with beautiful, violet-blue flowers from June to October. Midsummer heat does not deter the flowers and

the plants have mounds of deeply cut, green foliage that spread out. The foliage turns red in fall. Best of all, the blue color of the flowers deepens as the weather gets cooler.

The story of this remarkable plant began in Donald and Rozanne Waterer's garden in England in 1989. They were keen gardeners and had 25 to 30 different varieties of hardy geraniums planted in the garden. One day Rozanne noticed a plant that was different from the others. It was a strong grower, with large leaves and beautiful blue flowers. The next year this plant returned and flowered nonstop from June until November! Guess what they named it.

You can plant geranium 'Rozanne' in a cottage or rock garden. It makes a wonderful underplanting for roses. I find the purple flowers contrast beautifully with red or pink shrub roses. 'Rozanne' is also a lovely complement to the fluffy, buff-colored plumes of dwarf fountain grass (*Pennisetum alopecuroides* 'Hameln') in summer. Other flowering perennials that are good companions to geranium 'Rozanne' include lilies, veronica, and Shasta daisies, among many others.

Geranium 'Rozanne' is a sturdy perennial that is covered with beautiful, violet-blue flowers growing atop spreading, deeply cut, green foliage. It pairs beautifully with the flower plumes of dwarf fountain grass, shown here. Easy to grow. It reaches a height of 18 to 20 inches. It was named 2008 Perennial Plant of the Year by the PPA. Zones 5–8.

The profuse light purple blooms of geranium 'Rozanne' share a bed with pink 'Profusion' zinnias, an annual flower. A great combination.

Geranium 'Rozanne' can be planted above rocks and walls to great effect, spilling over them with abandon. 'Rozanne' is a perennial geranium that grows in full sun or partial shade (shade is preferred in southern regions of the United States). It likes good drainage, adequate water, and does not seem to be affected by insects or diseases. It is not eaten by rabbits. Not liked by deer.

Above: 'Yellow Meringue' false indigo (*Baptisia* 'Lemon Meringue') has lemon-yellow flowers on striking dark charcoal-colored stems. It has compact, well-branched foliage and grows 3 feet high and wide. The foliage is bluish-green and has a clover-like appearance. Baptisia does not transplant well and is long lived. It is deer resistant and combines well with bluestar (*Amsonia hubrichtii*) and ornamental native grasses. Zones 4–9.

Left: False indigo 'Cherries Jubilee' (*Baptisia* 'Cherries Jubilee') is a hybrid that is part of the Decadence series of baptisia. It has a shorter, more compact habit than the species. The deep maroon flower buds are held on strong stems above blue-green foliage, followed by masses of bicolor maroon and yellow flowers on upright branches in late spring to early summer. 'Cherries Jubilee' is stunning when combined with the soft, yellow flowers of baptisia 'Carolina Moonlight' and blue flowers of baptisia 'Purple Smoke,' as shown here. This is at the Coastal Maine Botanical Garden. Hardy in zones 4–9.

89. MAD FOR BAPTISIA!

A native perennial that is becoming more popular with each year is the deer-resistant baptisia (*Baptisia australis*), also known as false indigo. People are discovering this upright beauty and are appreciating it for its heat and drought tolerance, long life, resilience to pests, and handsome blue-green foliage and gorgeous pea-like flowers. It grows 3 to 4 feet tall, is sun loving, and does best in poor or lean soils. Baptisia flowers are borne on sturdy spikes in late spring to early summer. The flowers come in purple-blue, white, or yellow. They give way to 2- to 3-inch-long, blackish seedpods that rattle in the wind in late fall. Baptisia was the PPA 2010 Perennial Plant of the Year.

Baptisia is drought tolerant due to its long taproot and large root system that helps it survive long dry periods during the summer. But this feature also makes it hard to transplant. In other words, once you plant baptisia, it is very hard to move. Add to that is the fact that it grows large, almost like a shrub. You must be extra thoughtful about where you plant it! Baptisia can be grown as a backdrop in perennial borders or together in groups as a specimen planting for maximum effect. It is also suited for native or meadow plantings.

If you have a small outdoor space, it is a good idea to plant one of the baptisia cultivars that are more compact. The Decadence baptisia series has bushy hybrids that come in a delicious array of colors. The flowers have a light fragrance. They grow to 2½ to 3 feet tall, and they are hardy in USDA zones 4–9.

Baptisia, a native plant, is a magnet for butterflies. It provides early season nectar to a variety of butterflies and pollinators. It is also important as a food source for the caterpillars of orange sulphur, eastern tailed-blue, and wild indigo dusky wing butterflies.

The native white wild indigo (*Baptisia alba*) has unusual charcoal-gray stems and pea-like white blossoms on erect spikes above mounded blue-green foliage. It blooms from May to July and attracts and hosts numerous insects including the wild indigo dusky wing and orange sulfur caterpillars. It grows up to 4 feet tall in full sun. After the first frost, the entire shrub-like plant turns black, adding a stunning contrast to grasses and native goldenrod in late fall. Zones 4–9.

90. JAPANESE ANEMONES— STARS OF THE FALL GARDEN

I love late-season gardens, and I especially love the flowers that bloom in late summer and early fall. My favorites, besides chrysanthemums and asters, are the many cultivars of Japanese anemones (*Anemones* spp.). This easy-care perennial puts up elegant ball-shaped flower buds and has masses of dainty, daisy-like flowers in pink, lavender, and white with yellow centers borne on tall wiry stems. The flowers dance in the breeze, which is why it is also called windflower. Japanese anemones are relatively deer resistant with mounded foliage. It is one of my go-to plants. It is hardy from USDA zones 4–8.

Japanese anemones can grow to 4 feet tall, although there are shorter cultivars like the semi-double white anemone 'Whirlwind' that only grows 2 feet tall. A taller cultivar like the deep pink, double-flowered 'Bressingham Glow' grows to 4 feet tall and may need staking to keep from falling over. It is suitable for the back of a plant bed, against a picket fence, or in open woodlands, under trees. Fall-blooming anemones are quite lovely on their own in mass plantings and will spread via underground stems. Divide them every few years to keep them within their boundary.

Japanese anemones inject a colorful punch and are a sweet surprise when tucked in a shrub border. They like well-drained soil that stays moist, and they grow in part sun. They like a little afternoon shade, especially in the southern USDA hardiness zones.

Since Japanese anemones are stars in the fall, combine them with spring or summer bloomers to extend the season of your plant beds. Plant them with tulips, daffodils, hosta, bleeding heart, astilbe, allium, and hardy geranium. The graceful sprays of Japanese anemone flowers can also be blended with other late summer to early fall performers for a sensational display. Try them with sedum 'Autumn Joy,' asters, toad lily, coneflowers, goldenrod, and joe-pye weed.

'Honorine Jobert' Japanese anemone (*Anemone × hybrida* 'Honorine Jobert') is the most popular of all fall-blooming anemones. It is an heirloom white anemone hybrid with daisy-like flowers surrounding frilly yellow stamens. The flowers sit elegantly atop 3- to 4-foot-tall stems and bloom from late summer to fall. It is an easy-to-grow perennial. The sunny, glowing flowers brighten up early fall gardens for weeks. Zones 4–8.

Left: The Japanese anemone 'Honorine Jobert' (*Anemone × hybrida* 'Honorine Jobert') was named the 2016 Perennial Plant of the Year by the PPA. It does best when planted in partial shade or protected from hot afternoon sun. These tough perennials will naturalize and form a colony over time. Zones 4–8.

Below: 'Wild Swan' hybrid anemone is a prolific flowering anemone with huge white flowers from late spring to fall! It is different from Japanese anemones as it is an *Anemone rupicola* hybrid. It does not reseed and is noninvasive. It grows only 18 inches high and is 16 inches wide. It has a beautiful purple reverse, which is evident when flowers close at night. Part shade preferred. Zones 5–8. It is shown here growing with purple toad lilies (*Tricyrtis hirta*), a shade-tolerant perennial.

> ## "Flowers really do intoxicate me."
> ## —VITA SACKVILLE-WEST

'Gold Heart' bleeding heart has arching sprays of showy pink flowers with white tips in late spring. The flowers are the source of the plant's common name, including the little white droplet dripping out from the bottom. You can plant several 'Gold Heart' bleeding hearts together in a large planter where they will brighten a shady corner in spring. Plant with astilbe, ferns, and hellebores for a deer-resistant display.

91. "GOLD HEART" BLEEDING HEART

Bleeding heart (*Lamprocapnos spectabilis*) is a classic spring-blooming perennial. The cultivar known as 'Gold Heart' adds a special springtime zing to a landscape with its golden-yellow foliage. It positively glows in a shade garden while sporting the same nodding, puffy, heart-shaped pink flowers as the traditional bleeding heart. 'Gold Heart' is a wonderful addition to woodland gardens. Note: the leaves are chartreuse in shadier conditions and become less vibrantly colored as the season progresses. It grows to 2 feet tall, which is slightly smaller than the original bleeding heart. It is deer and rabbit resistant. It is suitable for USDA hardiness zones 6–9.

This quiet beauty likes the protected environment of a sheltered garden. Plant out of the way from high winds and exposed sites. 'Gold Heart' grows best in rich, loose soil that is moist and well drained. Do not plant in heavy, clay soils.

After its late spring floral display, 'Gold Heart' bleeding heart will go dormant in summer. For this reason, plant it with other shade-tolerant perennials and ferns to fill in the gaps later in the season. You can plant it in a mixed planting with coral bells (*Heuchera*), astilbe (*Astilbe*), maidenhair fern (*Adiantum*), hosta (*Hosta*), lungwort (*Pulmonaria*), and ligularia (*Ligularia*). Place it where you can enjoy the flowers up close.

The leaves of 'Gold Heart' bleeding heart (*Lamprocapnos spectabilis* 'Gold Heart') turn chartreuse in the shade of a woodland garden, as shown here. I planted it in a border of hostas and hellebores that grace a walkway. Every spring, the lovely arching wands appear, dangling pink bleeding heart flowers over the lichen-covered stones. It is native to Japan.

92. SIMPLE "DAY'S EYE"—SHASTA DAISY

The Shasta daisy (*Leucanthemum × superbum*) is summer personified. This garden staple has large white flowers that appear in early summer and continue to bloom all season. And its round yellow center looks like the sun, giving it the name "day's eye" or daisy. Shasta daisy flowers have such a clean simplicity that it is a natural scene stealer. In addition, this plant is easy to grow, attracts butterflies, and is deer and rabbit resistant. It blends in brightly with other summer sun lovers such as daylilies, salvia, liatris, grasses, and foxgloves. It is suitable for USDA hardiness zones 4–9.

The first Shasta daisy hybrid was introduced by famed American horticulturist Luther Burbank more than a century ago. He followed that up with the well-known Alaska hybrid and many more. Today, there are more than 100 named cultivars of this hardy perennial. Some grow to 3 feet tall. Others are much shorter, such as 'Snowcap,' a compact plant of 18 to 24 inches; 'Little Miss Muffet,' which is only 8 to 12 inches tall but with full-sized creamy white flowers; and 'Daisy May,' which grows 1 to 2 feet tall.

The compact cultivar 'Banana Cream' (*Leucanthemum superbum* 'Banana Cream') is a compact wonder growing 18 inches tall and 24 inches wide. It has long-blooming, bright lemon-yellow flowers that mature into pastel yellow. It blooms profusely from late spring through the summer. The 'Banana Cream' Shasta daisy is ideal for small gardens, and it is suitable for USDA hardiness zones 5–9.

In 2003, the 'Becky' Shasta daisy was named the PPA Perennial Plant of the Year. Its showy white flowers have wider petals than the original Alaska hybrid, and the strong stems need no staking. Heat and humidity do not bother it. A favorite in garden borders and beds, it blooms from July to September if deadheaded. It makes an excellent cut flower, lasting a week or more. A vase full of Shasta daisies in summer makes everyone smile.

'Snowcap' Shasta daisy (*Leucanthemum × superbum* 'Snowcap') is a favorite in the garden due to its compact habit and big, beautiful single white daisies with yellow centers. 'Snowcap' grows up to 15 to 18 inches tall, which fits in with smaller gardens. It has resilient stems that stay upright. Grow Shasta 'Snowcap' in full sun to part shade in well-drained soil. You can plant it along with low-growing sedum, as shown here. It is an easy-care plant that attracts butterflies and is rabbit resistant. Zones 5–8.

'Becky' Shasta daisies (*Leucanthemum × superbum* 'Becky') claim the spotlight in midsummer when they start to bloom. They continue to flower until early fall if deadheaded. 'Becky' grows 3 feet tall and wide, thrives in full sun in moist, well-drained soil. It is drought tolerant and looks great with pink 'Profusion' zinnias, as shown here.

In this garden bed, I planted Shasta daisies along with annual blue salvia and pink New Guinea impatiens. Although these sturdy perennials can be planted by themselves, they make a great companion to other sun-loving flowers with their strong visual presence. Snowy white Shasta daisies enhance all the other colors in a garden.

93. ALLIUMS OF ALL KINDS

The gardening world has gone mad for alliums (*Allium* spp.) and their colorful rounded blooms. Otherwise known as ornamental onions, these deer- and rabbit-resistant flowers are easy to grow. Alliums come in a wide assortment of colors, sizes, and blooming times. You can have different allium varieties blooming in your garden from spring through fall. Please note that the flowers do not have an onion smell. The foliage, however, will give off an oniony scent when crushed. Pollinators don't mind—the clustered umbel flowers are a favorite of bees, butterflies, and other beneficial insects.

Looking like little birthday balloons, alliums add a little whimsy to your flower garden. With so many varieties, where do you start? I suggest the summer-blooming *Allium* 'Millenium' with its globes of rose-pink flowers that cover the plant. It won the PPA 2018 Perennial Plant of the Year. 'Millenium' has deep green grassy foliage about 6 to 8 inches tall. Its flower stems rise 15 to 20 inches above the foliage in July to August, and it grows in clumps. It likes full sun but will tolerate a little shade. *Allium* 'Millenium' can be planted during the growing season. It goes well with Japanese anemones, salvia, and coneflowers. It is suitable for USDA hardiness zones 5–8.

Alliums come in oval, spherical, or domed flower shapes. Some varieties have blooms like loose fireworks such as *Allium cernuum*, commonly called nodding wild onion. It is a Northeastern native plant with clusters of small, bell-shaped, dangling lilac-colored florets. The umbel flower nods down, and so the flowers that appear in early summer are best seen when planted in a mass on a slope. It grows 18 inches tall and has a long bloom period. Mix with short grasses or perennials in a sunny, well-drained area. This allium is deer resistant, and it is suitable for USDA hardiness zones 4–8.

Top, left: *Allium* 'Millenium' blooms in summer, along with dark pink coneflowers and blue salvia. Its rosy-pink orbs are held on strong stems and add a fun lollipop effect. It has short grassy foliage that blends well in established flower beds, so feel free to add a few, here and there. *Allium* 'Millenium' grows no taller than 20 inches in bloom, perfect for the front of a border, as shown here. A wonderful cut flower, fresh or dried. Deer resistant. Zones 5–8.

Top, right: 'Globemaster' allium grabs the spotlight when it blooms in late spring through early summer. A hardy allium, it is prized for its elegant, 8- to 10-inch-diameter globe-shaped flower heads of pinkish-purple atop 30- to 36-inch-high stems. Each flower head is made up of numerous star-shaped violet flowers. The seed heads persist after the flower has passed. They are bulbs and must be planted in the fall. They bloom year after year with minimal care. Zones 5–7.

Bottom, left: Nodding onions are planted in a group on a sunny grassy slope at the Center for Sustainable Landscapes at Phipps Conservatory and Botanical Gardens. These native flowers bloom in summer and mix well with coneflowers (*Echinacea purpurea*) and milkweed (*Asclepias tuberosa*) for a native summer garden.

Bottom, right: 'Purple Sensation' allium (*Allium aflatunense* 'Purple Sensation') has 4- to 5-inch-diameter globes of deep violet-purple florets from May–June. They flower at the same time as late tulips, so try planting them together in the fall as I did here. They will continue blooming after the tulips have passed. 'Purple Sensation' grows 24 to 30 inches tall and is the first of the big purple allium globes to flower in the garden. It is a great cut flower. Zones 4–7.

94. A VERTICAL PUNCH—HARDY PERENNIAL SALVIA

If you want a dependable, beautiful, and care-free perennial with vertical flower spikes in your garden, look to the hardy perennial salvias—in particular, *Salvia nemorosa* and its many hybrids. Typically referred to as woodland sage or meadow sage, these deer- and rabbit-resistant herbaceous flowers have dense upright spikes of white, purple, or pink flowers. They are a favorite of bees, hummingbirds, and butterflies. Hardy salvia blooms like crazy from late spring into early summer, and it forms a low foliage mound that stays neat all season. No wonder these perennials are a staple in northern and central gardens.

Hardy salvia needs little attention. Once established in rich, well-draining soil, they can be in place for years without dividing. They prefer sunny spots for best flowering and are heat and drought tolerant. Best of all, hardy perennial salvia can be deadheaded to keep blooming, less robustly, later in the year. Once the flower stems have passed and turned brown, prune the stems down to where you see new buds forming on either side of the stem. A new set of flowers will appear in four to six weeks.

The spike flowers of hardy salvia work well with other early summer perennials that prefer dry, sunny conditions. These companions include coreopsis, yarrow, daylilies, catmint, dianthus, lady's mantle, and penstemons. Hardy salvia has many varieties to choose from. You can start with the well-known cultivar 'May Night' (*Salvia nemorosa* 'May Night'). Named PPA 1997 Perennial Plant of the Year, it is favored for its long-blooming, deep purple flowers and its pest and disease resistance. Other cultivars of *Salvia nemorosa* are the pink 'Eveline,'

the compact, white-blooming 'Snow Hill,' and the 'Blue Marvel,' which has extra-large blossoms of deep lavender-blue. All salvia flowers attract butterflies. It is a worthwhile addition to any pollinator garden.

Above: 'May Night' perennial salvia (*Salvia nemorosa* 'May Night') is a hardy cultivar known for its deep blue-purple blooms that remain upright. It has numerous dense flower spikes. Zones 4–8.

Opposite page: The hardy salvia hybrid 'Rhapsody in Blue' (*Salvia × sylvestris* 'Rhapsody in Blue') blooms in profusion at the remarkable Coastal Maine Botanical Garden. This clump-forming perennial grows to 18 to 24 inches tall with brilliant blue-violet spike flowers in early summer. It is very effective in drifts, as shown here. Zones 4–8.

95. THE DEPENDABLE ASTILBE

There is a good reason why astilbe is the traditional perennial flower for half-shade gardens—it is dependable, beautiful, and easy to grow. Known for mounds of ferny foliage and flower plumes rising on slender, upright, or arching stems, astilbes come in flower colors that include white, pink, red, and reddish purple. Astilbes have many hybrid varieties that vary in size, height, type of flower, and time of bloom. You can have short astilbes in front, and in the rear of the garden bed have 3-foot-tall varieties, such as 'Purple Candles.' All are deer resistant and thrive in part-shade, well-watered conditions.

Astilbes are the backbone of part-shade gardens. They make quite a show when planted in a large mass. You can also combine them with other moisture-loving shade plants such as ferns, Japanese forest grass, hellebore, brunnera, and hosta. For the front of a border, plant a group of short, 12-inch-high 'Sprite' dwarf astilbe (*Astilbe simplicifolia* 'Sprite') with its elegant, bronzy leaves.

This astilbe has feathery, shell-pink plumes in mid- to late summer. It was named the PPA 1994 Perennial Plant of the Year. In fall, its rust-colored seed heads are notable.

To create a garden with extended astilbe bloom, select several varieties with different bloom times. For example, for a late spring or early summer bloom time, plant 'Fanal' astilbe with its deep red blooms and 'Rheinland' astilbe, which has panicles of clear pink flowers on upright, reddish stems that grow to 24 inches tall. They bloom for two to three weeks. For blooms in midsummer, try the purple-plumed Amethyst astilbe and the pure white 'Deutschland' astilbe.

Late summer astilbes include the fluffy purple plumes of dwarf Chinese astilbe (*Astilbe chinensis* var. *pumila*). Astilbes also make wonderful dried flowers. Leave a few spent flower blossoms on the plants and enjoy the brown spikes through much of the winter.

Left: Astilbes look best in groups, and the fernlike foliage stays fresh-looking throughout the summer. Here, the airy flowers of astilbe 'Deutschland' (*Astilbe × arendsii* 'Deutschland') are planted in a large mass. The flowers reach 2 feet tall, adding drama to the landscape. The flowers are excellent for cutting. These midsummer bloomers blends well with columbine (*Aquilegia*), bleeding heart (*Lamprocapnos*), and Siberian bugloss (*Brunnera*). Astilbe resists diseases, slugs, and deer. Zones 4–9.

Right: Astilbe 'Rheinland' is one of the most beautiful astilbes, especially when planted in mass, as shown here. Its plume flowers are a showy, clear rose-pink above dark green, finely cut foliage. Blooms in early to midsummer to 24 inches tall. 'Rheinland' looks striking at a woodland edge, in a shade garden, or by a pond. Deer resistant. Zones 3–9.

Above: 'Golden Jubilee' giant hyssop (*Agastache rugosa* 'Golden Jubilee') combines golden yellow foliage with lavender-blue flowers. It is an upright perennial that grows to 2 to 3 feet tall. It is native to Asia. Fragrant, tubular, violet-pink flowers bloom summer–fall atop strong, rigid stems. Pinch in June to keep plants full and compact if desired. Zones 5–9.

Left: The raspberry-red tubular flowers of 'Tutti Frutti' hyssop (*Agastache* 'Tutti Frutti') loom over the garden on 3- to 4-feet-tall spikes from July–September. The flowers have a long bloom period and attract hummingbirds, butterflies, and other insects. Trim spent blossoms and more blooms will appear later in the growing season. Zones 6–9.

96. AGASTACHE—A POLLINATOR'S DELIGHT

One of the most attractive plants to pollinators is *Agastache,* also called hyssop or hummingbird mint. The popular perennial anise hyssop (*Agastache foeniculum*) is native to fields of eastern North America, and it gets its common name from its aromatic leaves that smell like licorice when crushed. Anise hyssop grows 2 to 4 feet tall, is deer resistant, and produces upright, 3- to 6-inch-long cylindrical lavender flower spikes from summer into fall. It produces large amounts of pollen and nectar, making it a favorite of bumblebees, honeybees, butterflies, and hummingbirds. It is drought tolerant and a vigorous grower. It is suitable for USDA hardiness zones 4–9.

Anise hyssop prefers full sun, good air circulation, and lean, dry soil. They do not require much water or fertilizer. The plants get floppy when grown in soil that is too rich. Plant it in the background of a sunny pollinator or native garden. Leave room for air to circulate. Plants self-sow readily. You can plant them with summer blooming grasses such as switchgrass, feather reed grass, milkweed, yarrow, gaillardia, or Russian sage.

Agastache hybrids come in a variety of colors, including shades of red, orange, pink, yellow, and white. Some popular hybrids are a cross between warm climate Agastache species, and so they are suited to USDA hardiness zones 7 and 8. There are many to choose from, including 'Apricot Sunrise,' with tubular, orange-apricot flowers that bloom nonstop from summer through early fall. They are typically 18 inches tall.

The soft, lavender-blue, bottlebrush-like flowers of 'Blue Fortune' Agastache (*Agastache* 'Blue Fortune') are borne on strong, 36-inch-tall upright stems from midsummer to early fall. This hybrid variety is cold hardy and tolerant of wet spring soils. It also tolerates heat and drought once established. Zones 5–8.

97. CRAZY FOR CONEFLOWERS

Coneflowers, also known as *Echinacea*, are one of our best-loved native perennial flowers. It is a prairie plant, native to the eastern and central United States, and makes the classic summer garden statement with its daisy-like blooms. Coneflowers light up sunny flower beds in midsummer through early fall, and they mix well with flowers and grasses alike. They are suitable for USDA hardiness zones 5–8. It is also an excellent cut flower.

The steadfast coneflower is striking when planted in a large group. After the flowers fade, the domed seed heads stand erect through the winter, attracting chickadees and goldfinches. In early spring, cut the flower stalks back. They need a sunny location and well-drained soil. There's no need to apply too much fertilizer. After about four years, dig up and divide the roots to keep plants vigorous. This is a great way to make new plants.

Purple coneflower (*Echinacea purpurea*) is the best known of the coneflowers. It has slightly drooping pink-purple petals surrounding a prickly copper-orange central cone. It is tough, and heat and drought tolerant once established.

A popular variety of this native coneflower is the bold 'Magnus,' which is hardy to USDA zone 4. It has magenta-rose flowers with petals that do not droop. Others to try include the All-America Selections (AAS) winner, PowWow® 'Wild Berry' coneflower, and the Pixie Meadowbrite coneflower. The latter grows only 8 to 20 inches tall. This smaller version of purple coneflower is suited to small spaces and an all-native landscape.

Piet Oudolf, the Dutch plantsman, uses coneflowers in his famed flower gardens. One of the selections he plants is the 'Fatal Attraction' coneflower (*Echinacea purpurea* 'Fatal Attraction'). It is a compact coneflower that blooms a little later than others. It has large, purple-pink flowers. Each flower has an orange-tinged purple cone surrounded by long, pointed petals and sits atop a dark red stem. It is suitable for USDA hardiness zones 3–8. Another coneflower that Oudolf plants is the 'Vintage Wine' (*Echinacea purpurea* 'Vintage Wine'), which was found in his garden in Holland. It looks great with Russian sage and liatris!

Top, left: 'Cheyenne Spirit' coneflower (*Echinacea* 'Cheyenne Spirit')
is a great cultivar of our native coneflower. This hybrid perennial won
the prestigious All-America Selections (AAS) award. It is grown from
seed and boasts rich shades of cream, golden yellow, orange, magenta,
and tomato-red. Each plant blooms one color, so plant in groups for a
riotous display. 'Cheyenne Spirit' plants are sturdy and bloom in mid-
to late summer on 18- to 24-inch-tall plants. Full sun. Zones 4–9.

Top, right: 'Double Scoop Bubble Gum' coneflower (*Echinacea
purpurea* 'Double Scoop Bubble Gum') has deep pink central cushions
of short petals that are surrounded by lighter pink petals. The name
describes the color of the 4-inch flowers perfectly! This upright plant
has sturdy stems—no staking required. Plant 'Double Scoop Bubble
Gum' with the white pompon flowers of the Pearl (*Achillea ptarmica*
Pearl) yarrow, as shown. Try 'Peter Cottontail' yarrow for this pairing.
It also looks great with Shasta daisies, blue salvias, and other 'Double
Scoop' colors—Cranberry, Orangeberry, and Raspberry coneflowers.
Blooms early to late summer. Zones 4–9.

Left: 'Mellow Yellows' coneflower (*Echinacea purpurea* 'Mellow Yellow')
produces lovely, long-lasting blooms that range from palest cream
to soft canary yellow. The flowers have darker cones, making them a
standout. Pollinators love it. Grows to 32 inches high. Zones 4–8.

Left: 'Gateway' joe-pye weed (*Eutrochium purp. maculatum* 'Gateway') is a robust, 6-feet-tall plant that does not need staking. Its large, deep pink flowers appear from July–September on wine-red stems. The showy flowers are a magnet for butterflies! It is best planted in full sun and rich, moist soils. Try the smaller joe-pye weed cultivars in tight or contained landscapes. Zones 4–8.

Right: Joe-pye weed flowers are eye-catching as they form in the midsummer. To keep these native plants bushy and with a shorter habit, cut them back in late spring before flowers form. It is a good background plant and combines well with tall native grasses and native flowers like black-eyed Susan, oxeye sunflower, ironweed, and Venusta queen of the prairie.

98. A NATIVE PERENNIAL TO TRY—JOE-PYE WEED

The verdict is in—plant more native flowering perennials! Gardens with non-native species of plants are often demanding of care and water and are of little benefit to wildlife. Native plants, on the other hand, are tough, suited to the region from which they came, and require little fertilizer to grow. They also use less water than exotic flowering perennials due to their deep root systems. Native plants can significantly reduce water runoff, as well. Best of all, they support our endangered pollinators and provide shelter and food for wildlife. Native plants are part of the natural ecosystem, and they attract more birds, bees, and butterflies than non-native plants.

There are other reasons for planting natives in your yard. They are long-lived, offer three- to four-season interest, and can reduce weeds by their dense groupings. With all that, who wouldn't want native perennials in their gardens?

Joe-pye weeds and their relatives are not well known, but they are one of the best native plants for attracting an assortment of butterflies to a late-season garden. They have long-blooming, large airy flowers, possess bold foliage, and come in a wide range of plant sizes. Some of them can grow to be 7 feet tall, making them a good screen or backdrop plant. They like moist, almost wet soils. A popular variety is 'Gateway' joe-pye weed (*Eutrochium purp. maculatum* 'Gateway'), which grows 4 to 6 feet tall and has dusky pink flowers from midsummer to early fall. Shorter hybrids include 'Little Joe' (*Eutrochium dubium* 'Little Joe'). It grows up to 5 feet tall, and it features enormous dome-shaped heads of rosy-purple flowers atop dark purple stems in late summer. It is easy to grow, but do not let it dry out. It's a magnet for butterflies. Leave the dried seed heads on the plant for winter interest.

"Beauty surrounds us, but usually we need to be walking in a garden to know it."
—RUMI

A SELECTION OF FAVORITE ANNUAL FLOWERS

Annual flowers, as their name implies, bloom in one year but do not come back the next. They must be planted anew each spring. This extra effort and cost cause some gardeners to dismiss annual flowers entirely. They note that some annuals require more watering, more fertilization, and are more prone to insect attack than perennial flowers (flowers that come back every year). In addition, some gardeners say that certain annuals may need to be deadheaded or "tipped back" in summer. This is all true. So why, then, do annual flowers make up the bulk of all plants currently sold?

Perhaps it is because annual flowers bloom relentlessly. Their task is to flower and get pollinated, and they typically bloom all season until frost, providing a constant display of color and form. They are floral workhorses. So while native perennial flowers may be the foundation of your garden, annuals can bridge any gaps in blooming between the perennial spring and summer bloomers. There is always something to look at when annuals are planted in a garden.

The answer, therefore, is to plant annual flowers that are tough, sturdy, and water-efficient. Yet still, annuals do cost money to buy every year. Growing them indoors from seeds in the late winter is a good way to get around that hurdle.

The best reason I can give for growing annuals, besides their glorious display, is that they are a good way to feed our bees, butterflies, and other beneficial insects. Some annuals are loaded with pollen and nectar, which draws pollinators to them. There are annual flower varieties, however, that are bred for showy flowers or vigorous growth; therefore, if you want to plant a pollinator garden, choose your flowers wisely. Some of the best annuals for attracting pollinators are cosmos, zinnia, alyssum, sunflower, marigold, petunia, lantana, pansies, ageratum, salvia, and pentas. Please note that lantana and pentas are considered annuals in northern states but are perennials in more southern states.

Many annual flowers are easy to grow, and they can really change the look of your outdoor space. You can experiment with color, fragrance, and form without committing to it beyond one growing season. So try growing some annual flowers, have fun, and enjoy the show you have created. The pollinators will thank you.

Which annual flowers should you start with? A good place to look is at the winners from All-America Selections (AAS), a trusted independent testing organization. These winners are garden varieties of flowers, vegetables, herbs, and plants that have been tested and proven to be excellent for home garden use by horticulture professionals across North America. It is a program run by the National Garden Bureau (ngb.org). A great list of the AAS Winners can be found on the AAS website (all-americaselections.org/winners).

The following are a few of some of my favorite annual flowers. I have highlighted some of them in previous sections of this book. There are so many annuals I like that it was hard to cull from the large group. I hope my choices whet your appetite to try many more in your garden.

Left: "Before" and "after" photos of a sunny border consisting of roses and annual flowers. This planting provides a nonstop colorful display all summer into fall.

Opposite page: A sunny annual flower border of spikes of lavender angelonia, yellow French marigolds, pink annual vinca, and purple ageratum on the left. All deer resistant!

99. HOT HOT HOT!

Do you want a vibrant annual flower bed that is easy to grow and turns heads? If you have a sunny spot, try growing a combination of Zinnia 'Profusion Double Hot Cherry,' Zinnia 'Double Zahara Fire,' and 'Summer Jewel Red' tropical sage. The fiery hues are hot, hot, hot!

Zinnia 'Profusion Double Hot Cherry' (*Zinnia interspecific hybrid*) is a mounded, 8- to 14-inches-high solid performer. An award-winning annual with vividly colored, multi-petaled blooms of deep rose flowers, it blooms from summer through frost. It is deer resistant, drought tolerant, and stands up to the heat of summer with no color fading. It is the 2013 AAS Bedding Plant Winner.

Zinnia 'Double Zahara Fire' (*Zinnia marylandica* 'Double Zahara Fire') features large, fiery, orange, double-petaled flowers. This AAS award winner is fade resistant and easy to grow. It reaches 1 to 2 feet in height and is adored by hummingbirds, butterflies, and birds. It is a great cut flower for mini bouquets.

The red flower spikes of 'Summer Jewel Red' tropical sage (*Salvia coccinea* 'Summer Jewel Red') is a magnet for hummingbirds. This is why it's also called hummingbird sage. It grows to 20 inches tall and stands up to wind and rain.

Top: Plant these three flowers together—the lower-growing, mounded Zinnia 'Profusion Double Hot Cherry' in front of both 'Double Zahara Fire' zinnia and 'Summer Jewel Red' tropical sage for a summer-long fiery display!

Bottom: 'Summer Jewel Red' tropical sage blooms early on densely branched, compact plants. Besides attracting hummingbirds, its seeds are a favorite of goldfinches.

Above: Zinnia 'Profusion Double Hot Cherry' is a durable, easy-care flower. It loves full sun and freely draining, humusy soil. It does not require deadheading. Resistant to powdery mildew.

Left: 'Double Zahara Fire' zinnia features densely petaled orange flowers that don't fade. These flowers grow 14 inches tall and are mildew resistant and vigorous. Withstands summer humidity like a champ. It is a 2010 AAS Bedding Plant Winner.

100. WHY VAN GOGH LOVED SUNFLOWERS

"I find comfort in contemplating the sunflowers."
—VINCENT VAN GOGH

Vincent van Gogh, the 19th-century Dutch artist, is famous for his paintings of sunflowers. He loved them so much that he painted a total of 12 sunflower still life paintings. What was the aspect of annual sunflowers (*Helianthus annuus*) that enticed van Gogh? He admired their vibrant yellow color, their bold form, and the fact that they are sturdy, common plants (he called them the "rustic" sunflower). But there was another reason that made him paint depictions of cut sunflowers in a vase.

Vincent van Gogh saw the sunflower's floral solar disc as something of a symbol. According to the Van Gogh museum in Amsterdam, he wrote that the sunflower paintings communicated "gratitude." He felt that the simple, sun-like image of the common sunflower conveys the powerful idea of Nature's bounty and beauty itself. Indeed, the National Gallery in London, England, reports that its sunflower still life by van Gogh is one of their most popular paintings. It is this artwork that is most often reproduced on cards, posters, mugs, and stationery in their store. It seems we all respond to the happiness of sunflowers and their message of Nature's glory!

There are many varieties of annual sunflowers, including dwarf and tall varieties. The bloom colors range from bright yellow to lemon yellow to orange, pink, and even burgundy. And there are those that are grown especially for seed harvesting, like 'Super Snack Mix,' which has a solitary 10-inch-wide flower on a 5-foot-tall plant.

Annual sunflowers are easy to grow from seed if you have full sun and growing room. Sunflowers are warm-weather plants, so wait until the soil has warmed to at least 55 degrees before sowing seeds. Sunflowers do best in a spot sheltered from the wind. For a longer sunflower bloom period, plant a row or group of sunflowers every two weeks for four to six weeks during the early summer. They make a great cut flower. Grow a lot of them and you can have a vase full of sunflowers, just like Vincent painted.

Sunflowers are easy to grow, and are a perfect flower for a children's garden.

101. WHAT IS A BEDDING PLANT?

Annual flowers are often planted in specially prepared garden beds for a seasonal display. For this reason, they are called bedding plants. Home gardeners in the United States do not use the term *bedding plant*, but it is a handy way to describe the planting of fast-growing plants in flower beds to create colorful and temporary displays. Low-growing annual flowers, tender perennials, and succulents such as sedums can all be used for this purpose.

"Bedding" may be associated with elaborate public gardens, but the name can be applied to any decorative flower bed. This includes street planters, hotel lobbies, median strips, or even small front yards where a decorative punch is desired.

Bedding displays of annual plants are often changed two or three times a year. Professional gardeners may plant in late spring for summer shows, and then plant in early autumn for winter and/or spring displays. You can do this in your garden, too. First plant tulip bulbs in fall, then follow it up with pansies and sweet alyssum in early spring, and then plant late-blooming annuals or dahlias for late-summer interest—all in the same flower bed! I like planting angelonia, annual blue salvia, gomphrena, or zinnias for summer and/or fall color in a bed. It requires planning, but bedding-plant succession ensures a constant floral show outdoors.

Multicolored gomphrena are planted in beds in the traditional carpet bedding that was popular in Victorian times. This is at Mohonk Mountain House, a hotel in New Paltz, New York. Deer resistant.

102. PRAISE FOR PANSIES

Pansies (*Viola × wittrockiana*), with their heart-shaped, overlapping petals and their wide range of bright colors and patterns, are cool-weather favorites that can survive a light frost. You can find these versatile cottage garden flowers providing a burst of color in both early spring and late fall gardens. They are really biennials. They are sold in their second year, when blooming, and are grown as annuals. These low-growing beauties make great companions to spring flowering bulbs such as daffodils and wood hyacinths. They are also an early food source for insects. Unfortunately, pansies are not deer resistant.

The English nobleman William Thompson bred the first modern pansies in the early 1800s from the wildflower *Viola tricolor* and the horned violet *Viola cornuta*. In it, he saw a "miniature impression of a cat's face." The blotched, cheerful "faces" of these flowers have captivated children and adults alike ever since, and they have charmed their way into our hearts. Pansies now enjoy new popularity as the perfect edible adornment to many culinary dishes and desserts.

Modern gardeners can choose from hundreds of pansy varieties, from trailing ones like 'Cool Wave' and 'Waterfall' to antique ones such as 'Imperial Antique Shades,' with their soft color tones that range from apricot to rose. Some varieties of pansies are pure black and others are pure yellow, such as 'Matrix Yellow Clear' Pansy. Pansies are treated as cool-weather annuals, but the new varieties have increased strength and are more heat tolerant than older varieties. Hardy varieties include the Sky series, Delta series, and Accord series, among others.

To get the best from pansies, keep them moist and cool, and use an organic slow-release, balanced fertilizer to maximize flowering. They grow well in full sun, although they may continue to bloom into summer if planted in some shade. To keep flowers blooming, clip them frequently and deadhead faded blooms.

Make sure pansies are planted in a well-drained location. Tuck them around perennial plants that thrive in part shade, such as coral bells (*Heuchera*). Plant a few colorful pansies in a pot by your door in early spring and you will smile every time you pass by.

Top, left: Light blue pansies with darker centers and yellow eyes are very effective when planted in groups and tucked in and around daffodil foliage. Here, they contrast beautifully with Siberian wallflower 'Citrona Yellow' (*Erysimum allionii* 'Citrona Yellow').

Top, right: Cream-colored pansies blend with darker yellow violas and pastel-colored wood hyacinths in front.

Bottom, left: I planted purple pansies to complement the frosted leaves and light blue flowers of 'Jack Frost' brunnera (*Brunnera macrophylla* 'Jack Frost'), commonly known as bugloss. The mix of the dainty forget-me-not flowers of the perennial brunnera with the happy faces of the pansies are a charming blend. Brunnera grows in zones 3–8.

Bottom, right: Ruffled or frilled pansies are so charming, especially when planted in a vintage, slightly rusted urn. They are so impressive when planted in the cool weather of early spring!

103. NEW GUINEA IMPATIENS—A GO-TO FLOWER

If you have only half-day sun in your garden, do not despair. New Guinea impatiens will light up the partially shaded space, even if you only tuck a few plants here and there in the plant beds. These reliable, easy-to-grow, colorful flowers will bloom like crazy until fall. To be clear, they are not the same as the common shade-loving impatiens (*Impatiens walleriana*) that we all know. New Guinea impatiens are not susceptible to the fungus called impatiens downy mildew that has afflicted common impatiens across the country. For this reason, you can plant New Guinea impatiens as a substitute for common impatiens in part-shade beds and planters.

New Guinea impatiens are known for their flashy flowers and remarkable leaf coloration and patterns. Some have leaves with swirls of yellow in the center; others have dark bronze leaves with red and orange markings. And the thick-petaled flowers, which can reach to 3 inches across, range from bright pink, white, red, purple, and lavender to flashy orange. The blooms come in solid colors and bicolored forms. They sport a flower spur full of nectar, which makes them a favorite of moths and butterflies. No deadheading is required, and they are relatively trouble-free. New Guinea impatiens need moist, well-drained soil—do not let them dry out but make sure the soil is not permanently wet. It does best in at least a half-day of full sun, preferably morning sun and afternoon shade.

One of the recent introductions is the sun-tolerant SunPatiens®, a hybrid of New Guinea impatiens. They do well in both sun and shade. SunPatiens® survives hot temperatures and intense sunlight, which is ideal for gardens in southern regions. Other cultivars include the Divine and Sonic® series. These are dense plants with leaves that grow right to the ground, and they are well suited for the front of a border or in large group plantings. New Guinea impatiens look great when planted with finer annuals such as euphorbia Diamond Snow® or taller spike flowers like angelonia.

Super Sonic ® 'Sweet Cherry' New Guinea impatiens (*Impatiens hawkeri* Super Sonic ® 'Sweet Cherry') shares a partially shaded bed with the attractive pink-and-green leaves of 'Magilla' perilla (*Perilla frutescens* 'Magilla'), a fast-growing, coleus-like foliage plant that does not seed or spread. The Super Sonic ® 'Sweet Cherry' New Guinea impatiens is an eye-catcher with its shell-pink round flowers and hot pink overtones with a blotch in the center. It grows 14 to 16 inches tall and can tolerate heat.

Three different colors of New Guinea impatiens mix well with the yellow-green foliage of Japanese forest grass 'All Gold.' The dark green leaves of the New Guinea impatiens set off the vividly colored flowers beautifully. Both do well in part sun conditions.

104. COMING UP COSMOS

If you wanted one annual to grow in a sunny garden, I would suggest the beautiful, daisy-like cosmos. It is one of the easiest flowers to grow from seed sown directly on the garden bed (after all danger of frost has passed). Its flowers come in a variety of bright colors and styles. You can plant 12-inch-high dwarf cosmos, or 4-feet-tall giants, and anything in between. The light flowers on wiry stems and feathery foliage add movement to the garden. Best of all, cosmos is top rated for attracting birds, bees, beetles, moths, and butterflies. It blooms from late spring to the first frost of fall. Pollinators love cosmos.

Cosmos need sun and heat, and they relish poor soil. Do not fertilize it at planting. Soil that is too rich will weaken their stems and diminish flowering. To keep the flowers growing, trim a third of the way down after the first bloom. The taller varieties of cosmos require protection from the wind. Lastly, give it air and room—they do best when not crowded.

A popular cosmos variety is 'Dwarf Early Sensation Mix' (*Cosmos bipinnatus* 'Dwarf Early Sensation Mix'). This prolific cosmos gives you an early start and grows to only 12 inches tall. Its large single flowers come in a variety of pinks and whites. Plant this rugged flower in the garden, meadow, or in planters. Lovely for early summer bouquets.

Sulphur Cosmos (*Cosmos sulphureus*) is a cosmos species that typically grows to 1 to 3 feet tall. It is native to Mexico, loves high temperatures, is drought tolerant, and is bushier than the classic wildflower cosmos. It has semi-double to double flowers that range from yellow to scarlet red. The popular 'Diablo' sulphur cosmos is a reddish orange and grows 24 to 36 inches tall. Dwarf Lemon sulphur cosmos grows just 18 to 30 inches tall and features lemon-yellow flowers. It looks great interplanted with perennials.

Left: The pure white, daisy-like blooms of 'Sonata White' cosmos (*Cosmos bipinnatus* 'Sonata White') draw butterflies by the dozen. The flowers are held atop wiry stems above feathery foliage on relatively low-growing plants. The long-lasting, compact white flowers are perfect for garden beds or containers. It's great in vases, too. The 24-inch-tall plants thrive in poor dry soils and can be mixed with other sun-loving annuals such as zinnias and tall verbena (*Verbena bonariensis*).

Opposite page: Cosmos Picotee is one of the most beautiful of all the beloved cosmos. Its white or pink flowers are edged with distinctive bright rose-red, and it has a vivid yellow center. Self-cleaning and easy to grow, these plants reach 3 to 5 feet tall and bloom from early summer until frost. It makes a striking backdrop in a flower bed. They are tough and do well in hot weather and poor soil. For a shorter but similar bicolor look, try the early-flowering 'Cosimo Purple Red-White' cosmos cultivar, which produces 18- to 24-inch-tall bushy plants.

105. AH, AGERATUM

If you want an annual with soft blue or lavender blooms, then the enduring favorite *Ageratum houstonianum* is ideal. Also known as floss flower, ageratum features dense clusters of powder puff, flowers covering mounded plants from May through October. This dependable plant, which is native to Central America, is deer-resistant, moderately drought tolerant but prefers fertile, well-drained soil and full sun.

The shorter varieties of ageratum grow no higher than one foot and are wonderful filler plants, blending with others well. Their mounded appearance makes them especially suited as edging along walks, in front of borders, and in pots and window boxes. They are also great in rock gardens. The taller varieties can be used in mid-borders or in cutting gardens.

Some low-growing, dwarf varieties of annual ageratum include 'Blue Danube,' which grows to 6 to 8 inches high, or the early flowering 'Blue Hawaii'. Others like 'Blue Blazer' and 'Royal Delft' grow to only 4 to 6 inches tall. The taller varieties such as Blue Horizon grow to 30 inches tall and are perfect cut flowers. A particular favorite is the 'Artist Blue' ageratum series. It thrives in full heat and full sun.

The soft blue flowers of ageratum combine well with pink in the garden, such as pink begonias, pink annual vinca, or pink lantana. Blue and yellow is another combination. Pair short yellow marigolds or yellow sulphur cosmos with tall blue ageratum for contrast. It is a great combination for sunny planters, too.

Here, I planted light blue ageratum as a facer flower in front of variegated boxwood. Behind the low shrubs are the upright delicate blooms of tall raspberry angelonia. Note the single plants of cherry-red annual vinca inserted occasionally in the bed. They add a colorful "pop" to the scene. This is a fun accent that can work anywhere. All deer resistant!

Left: Lavender-blue ageratum mixes beautifully with the tall spikes of summer snapdragon (*Angelonia angustifolia*). These two annuals make a stunning blue statement in the sunny landscape.

Right: Although various shades of blue are the most common colors of ageratum, pink and white selections are available to expand the possibilities. Now you can use white ageratum to accompany blue ageratum in a display.

106. SWEET POTATO VINE AMIDST THE FLOWERS

Sweet potato vine (*Ipomoea batatas*) is not an annual flower. It is grown for its colorful foliage and is an ornamental variety with a trailing habit. It does not provide the starchy edible potatoes. The leaves of these vigorous plants have striking colors and forms, and they make an effective seasonal ground cover in the flower garden. They are also wonderful spillers in containers, providing color all summer long. Sweet potato vine thrives in full sun or partial shade with ample moisture. They grow fast in heat and humidity. Foliage color is best on plants that receive afternoon shade. It is a perennial in USDA hardiness zones 9–11.

These eye-catching vines add a zing to established shrub borders and flower beds. The leaves come in shades of purple, chartreuse, red, bronze, and even multicolored. And their shapes range from lacy to heart shaped. The popular 'Blackie'

sweet potato vine (*Ipomoea batatas* 'Blackie'), which comes from the Proven Winners brand of plant propagators, has deeply lobed, blackish-maroon foliage that sets off any other flowering or foliage plant. It grows to 6 feet long and is a vigorous grower, making it great for filling a large area quickly. If it gets out of bounds, don't be afraid to clip the plant back. There is no need to fertilize it unless you want superfast growth.

There are more compact varieties of sweet potato vine that grow only to 30 inches long. These work especially well in containers. The popular 'Illusion Midnight Lace' sweet potato has finely cut, almost black, lacy foliage that forms more of a mound. It is easy to grow. Its chartreuse sister plant, 'Illusion Emerald Lace' sweet potato vine, is just as enchanting. Lastly, try 'Pink Frost,' which is remarkable for its tricolor leaves edged in pink. It blends well with pink flowers.

Top: 'Blackie' sweet potato vine fills in large garden areas with deep purple foliage. The foliage is a bold accent to flowering annuals such as 'Alaska Mix' nasturtium, with its unique variegated and marbled foliage and light orange, edible flowers. I also tucked in white New Guinea impatiens to cool it all off.

Bottom: 'Margarita' sweet potato vine (*Ipomoea batatas* 'Margarita') has bright chartreuse leaves that turn pale green in partial shade. The heart-shaped foliage brightens any bed! Here in a half-sunny bed, I planted a tapestry of foliage and flowers with 'Lemon Twist' Swedish ivy (*Plectranthus* 'Lemon Twist') and the pink and purple flowers of calibrachoa.

107. GOING WITH GOMPHRENA

I have always loved gomphrena, commonly known as globe amaranth, and its pink, purple, or white gumball flowers. They are solid, drought-tolerant bloomers, going nonstop from early summer until the first hard frost. Now, with the new hybrids developed from a cross with the heat-loving lanky Rio Grande globe amaranth (*Gomphrena globosa*), the range of gomphrena flower head colors have expanded to include red, pink, purple, lilac, orange, violet, and white. The hybrids also come in different heights, such as the Ping Pong® series that grows 16 to 20 inches high, making it easy to mingle them with others in the garden. As a bonus, gomphrena is a reliable cut flower and can be dried to make an everlasting bouquet. It's deer resistant, too!

The short mounding varieties of *Gomphrena globosa,* such as 'Buddy Purple,' 'Buddy Rose,' and 'Buddy White,' flower from late spring to mid-fall, with clover-like flower heads in violet-purple, rose, or white flowers respectively. They grow no higher than 1 foot tall and are typically planted at the front of a garden bed. 'Purple Gnome' gomphrena grows to only 6 to 10 inches. You can plant the short globe amaranth in early summer to fill in areas left open by spent spring bulbs or cool-season flowers.

Gomphrena works well in sunny planters for season-long color. The rich purple blooms make a great contrast to yellow, pink, and white heat-loving flowers such as lantana, zinnia, and marigolds. Taller cultivars can be inserted in a bed with annual blue salvia, coneflowers, and airy euphorbias. And you can dry the button-type flowers by cutting them, removing foliage, bunching loosely, and hanging them upside down in a cool, well-ventilated place.

The new gomphrena varieties include the showstopper *Gomphrena pulchella* 'Fireworks' and the long-stemmed, bright red *Gomphrena haagean* 'Strawberry Fields.' Both are heat loving and make great cut flowers that will have everyone talking.

'Fireworks 'gomphrena (*Gomphrena pulchella* 'Fireworks') has hot pink blooms that look as if they exploded with little rays of yellow. The abundant, drought-tolerant flowers seemingly float in the air on 3- to 4-foot-tall stems. The shorter 'Truffula Pink' gomphrena grows to 28 inches tall and is covered with similar hot pink flowers. No deadheading required. 'Truffula Pink' is perfect for containers in hot-sunny areas.

Above: The short 'Buddy Purple' gomphrena works well as an edging to Flower Carpet 'Pink Supreme' ground cover rose. The colors blend nicely and they both thrive in sunny, hot weather. As with other gomphrenas, the flowers invite pollinators such as bees, moths, and butterflies.

Left: QIS Series gomphrena is a mix of globose-type flowers in a range of colors and shades including the rare, orange-scarlet flowers. This popular mix is great for hot sunny beds or cut flowers. Grows 24 to 30 inches tall and the seed can be directly sown on the ground after all danger of frost has passed. Deer resistant.

108. ANGELONIA FOR ALL

If you are looking for a deer-resistant, heat-loving flower (perennial in frost-free climates) that comes in a palette of blues, pinks, purples, and white—go with angelonia. This flower is almost foolproof and laughs at hot and humid summers. It likes sun and moisture, and it is a magnet for butterflies and bees. It is suitable for USDA hardiness zones 9–11.

In the 1990s, the new compact angelonias came on the market. They were originally bred from gangly *Angelonia angustifolia*, a native to Mexico and the West Indies. Sometimes called summer snapdragon due to its two-lipped flowers and upright, spiky posture, angelonias are a great complement to other flowers. Most varieties are 12 to 18 inches high and can be used in flower beds, containers, and window boxes. They are a natural "thriller" plant for the center of a planter due to their upright nature and constant blooming.

There are many wonderful cultivars to try. The 'Angelface' series by the Proven Winners brand of plant propagators is semi-upright and has extra-large, brilliantly colored blooms. It grows around 2 feet high. 'Angelface' has a slight grape soda fragrance. The 'Archangel' series has exceptionally larger flowers and a well-branched habit with glossy dark green leaves. Its flower colors include raspberry, dark purple, coral, dark rose, and orchid pink.

The 'Serenita' series is exciting because it is a seed-propagated series with tough, long blooming plants that grow to only 10 to 14 inches tall. The 'Serenita' angelonia flowers are even more compact than the popular Serenas, and they have small fragrant narrow leaves, giving them a fine texture.

The pristine white blossoms of 'Archangel' white angelonia stand on tall stems in front of a hedge of clipped boxwood. It blooms happily from late spring until frost with little deadheading. Needs sun. I planted it here with blue ageratum as an edging. Boxwood, angelonia, and ageratum are all deer resistant.

Angelonia angustifolia, or summer snapdragon, is a vigorous flowering plant with upright spike flowers that may sprawl but do not need staking. It comes in a range of cool colors that brighten up summer flower beds. Angelonia is resistant to heat, drought, deer, and rabbits. It does not need deadheading. It also makes a great long-lasting cut flower.

Above: Butterflies and bees love zinnias. These nectar- and pollen-laden flowers will bloom until hard frost, providing food for beneficial pollinators for a long period. The bigger-flowered zinnias have petals that act like landing pads for butterflies. Tall hot pink zinnias seem to get the biggest draw.

Top, right: 'Queen Red Lime' zinnias (*Zinnia elegans* 'Queen Red Lime') have fully double flowers, up to 3 inches wide. They feature petals that shade from maroon at the base to lime green around the central cone. It inserts antique rose and vintage pink into a bed. This plant is tall and well branched. Grows up to 40 inches. It blooms until October.

Bottom, right: White and red zinnias are breathtaking in summer. The white blooms brighten up an evening garden under a full moon.

109. MUST-HAVE ZINNIAS

The annual summer flower that I love the most are zinnias. They come in myriad forms and colors, and all are dazzling. Better still, they love summer heat and stand up to drought. And they are so easy to grow! Zinnias can be seeded outdoors directly when all danger of frost has passed. Once it germinates, it goes to flower in a few weeks. They bloom all through the summer and into fall. You can seed a second batch a month later if you want continuous cut flowers.

If you like color and have a sunny spot, then zinnias are a must-have for you. They come in a range of bright and pastel colors, plus bicolors and tricolors. Here are just four of the many low-growing zinnias you might try:

- 'Zahara' zinnias grow to just 8 to 12 inches. They are resistant to powdery mildew and leaf spot. 'Zahara' comes in brilliant colors and are self-cleaning—no deadheading required.
- The 'Profusion' series of hybrid zinnias are also resistant to powdery mildew and need no deadheading. Zinnia 'Profusion' will grow up to 14 inches tall or a little shorter. Prized for its compact form, it features early and continuous blooms all season long.
- 'Lilliput' zinnia (*Zinnia elegans* 'Lilliput') is one of most popular zinnia varieties, due to its unique pompon flowers that come in a multitude of colors. It makes a great cut flower, grows 18 to 24 inches tall, and is easy to grow. Studies found that 'Lilliput' attracted twice the number of butterflies as other zinnia cultivars tested.

Zinnias are best known as the tall-growing flowers that everyone loves to cut. They can grow up to 3 feet tall. Try the 'Benary's Giant' zinnia, which has sturdy stems and large flowers. There is also the popular 'Cut and Come Again' and 'State Fair' zinnias. I must admit my favorite is the award-winning 'Queen' series zinnias with their unusual color combinations and thickly layered petals in semi-double and double flowers. These vigorous plants grow to 40 inches high on strong stems.

110. EDIBLE NASTURTIUMS

Have you ever eaten nasturtiums? These beautiful, trumpet-shaped flowers make a delicious garnish that adds color and a peppery taste to any salad; the soft petals are similar to the taste of a radish. Add the colored blossoms to an open-faced sandwich, use as a garnish for an omelet, or add some zing to your potato salad. And the young, edible leaves contain high levels of vitamin C. Nasturtiums (*Tropaeolum majus*) certainly add a floral flourish to a summer meal.

Nasturtiums are fast-spreading, sun-loving annuals that are easy to grow. The circular leaf adds a striking aspect of this annual flower as the leaves resemble round lily pads and are eye-catching in a garden bed or planter. Sow seeds in the ground or in containers. They prefer poor soil, so no added fertilizer is necessary. Note that fertile soil will result in fewer blooms and more foliage!

The popular dwarf, bushy varieties of nasturtium have dense foliage and sport glorious flowers. Use them in a planter or at the front of a border. 'Tom Thumb' dwarf nasturtium grows into an 8- to 12-inch-tall mound. Another wonderful dwarf is Nasturtium 'Tip Top Rose,' a 2020 All America Selections Flower Winner. It has unique, rose-colored flowers on 14- to 18-inch-tall mounded plants.

You can also try 'Empress of India,' an heirloom nasturtium with deep blue-green foliage and vermilion-red blossoms. The red flowers attract hummingbirds that love to visit the long-spurred blossoms. Finally, try planting tall-climbing nasturtium vines on a pole or trellis. These produce bigger flowers than the dwarf and semi-trailing species. Popular varieties include 'Jewel of Africa' and 'Tall-Trailing Mix.'

Nasturtium flowers and their round green leaves make an appealing display in a wooden salad bowl. These add a distinct peppery flavor to salads, soups, and sandwiches. *Photo by Steven Edgar Bradbury.*

'Alaska Mix' nasturtium has gold, yellow, orange, salmon, and deep red flowers that peek out from attractive cream-and-green marbled foliage. The compact plants grow 10 to 16 inches tall. Best in sun and poor soil.

List of Public Gardens

Here is an alphabetical listing of the public gardens mentioned or illustrated in *Floratopia*. I encourage you to add these remarkable places to your bucket list when traveling. Make sure they are open on the day you want to visit.

Berkshire Botanical Garden, Stockbridge, Massachusetts

Bridge of Flowers, Shelburne Falls, Massachusetts

Coastal Maine Botanical Gardens, Boothbay Harbor, Maine

Elisabeth C. Miller Botanical Gardens, Seattle, Washington

Epcot International Flower & Garden Festival, Walt Disney World, Orlando, Florida

Harry P. Leu Gardens, Orlando, Florida

Mohonk Mountain House (a resort hotel), New Paltz, New York

Monet's Garden, Giverny, France

New York Botanical Garden, Bronx, New York

Phillis Warden (private garden), Bedford Hills, New York (Open Days program of The Garden Conservancy)

Phipps Conservatory and Botanical Gardens, Pittsburgh, Pennsylvania

Rhododendron Species Botanical Garden, Federal Way, Washington

Steinhardt (private garden), Mount Kisco, New York (Open Days program of The Garden Conservancy)

Stonecrop Gardens, Cold Spring, New York

Wave Hill, Bronx, New York

Index

Page numbers in *italics* refer to illustrations.

W

X

Y

Z